WINTER IN THE CITY OF LIGHT

SUE HARPER

A SEARCH FOR SELF IN RETIREMENT

Cathryn

Without you this book would not exist. Thanks for the help with self-publishing and for your invaluable insights.

Sue

Harper, Sue 1952 –, author
Winter in the City of Light: A Search for Self in Retirement / Sue Harper

ISBN: 978-1-9995652-0-6 (ebook)
ISBN: 978-1-9995652-1-3 (print)

Book Design: Friction Creative
Cover Image: © Bonnie Sheppard

The names of some people featured in this book have been changed
to protect their privacy.

FOR BONNIE – THOU

PRAISE

"This is a memoir that reminds us that each new phase of life asks us to start again. Facing the long quiet of retirement and hours of solitude while her partner burrows happily into her art, Sue Harper rediscovers her courage, herself, and her love of history as she explores Paris on her own and delves into some of its most iconic stories and characters. Accompanied by useful tidbits of information about neuroscience and psychology, this is a book that not only shows us how life really and truly begins at 60-something, it makes us want to hurry up and get there so we can begin too."

Jane Silcott author of *Everything Rustles* co-editor of *Love Me True: Writers Reflect on the Ins, Outs, Ups and Downs of Marriage*

"A must-read for Gen Xers like me who are approaching retirement and wondering what that will look like. Harper's Winter in the City of Light makes it beautifully clear that this stage of one's life can be as creative as any other. A remarkably well-written book that I promise you won't be able to put down."

S. Lesley Buxton author of *One Strong Girl: Surviving the Unimaginable: a Mother's Memoir* (winner of the Pottersfield Prize for Non-fiction)

"Boomers seeking for themselves a consultable reference book for retirement (a la Dr. Spock's Common Sense Book of Baby and Child Care) are in luck. Sue Harper's insightful, well-observed, warts-and-all memoir about her retirement adventures (and how she nurtured her inner flâneuse while learning to value the journey over the destination) offers a non-prescriptive walk-with-me guidebook to the often bumpy ride that is life's much misunderstood third act. And it's a delightful read, to boot, taking the reader through a well-limned season in Paris."

Moira Dann author, journalist, and editor of the bestselling *Facts&Arguments: Selected Essays from The Globe and Mail (Penguin)*

TABLE OF CONTENTS

CHAPTER 1

RETIREMENT IN BLACK AND WHITE: CRISIS POINT

"I'm going to follow in the footsteps of writers like Hemingway. I'll become a *flâneur*, or rather a *flâneuse*, walk the city and write," I boasted.

Of course, it was a lie.

We were in Paris. While my partner, Bonnie, drew nudes in the first studio of Henri de Toulouse-Lautrec and Baroque sculptures in the vaulted galleries of the Louvre Museum's Cour Puget, I sat in our rented apartment, my head aching, my heart pounding, my intestines twisted in knots, afraid to step out into a city where I had trouble speaking the language and where, thanks to urban planner Georges-Eugène Haussmann, the streets all looked the same.

Even as I write this, I realize that, to most, the chance to spend nine weeks in Paris, alone, free of timelines and schedules, would be a dream, a fantasy, a lottery win.

Not to me.

Leading up to the trip, I had nightmares. Hemingway spent a great deal of his time in Paris drunk. While that might be one option for calming the rising panic I felt just thinking of travelling alone for the first time in Bonnie's and my thirty-five years together, I didn't want to admit my apprehension. I knew my retirement looked ideal, but I was not coping.

"What are you going to do?" is a malicious question, one I heard over and over before I retired. If I had said "nothing," would that have been acceptable? Of course, that was never an option – not for a goal-oriented person like me. My answer remained steadfast. "We've got it worked out. Bonnie is going to paint, and I'm going to write." I had no reason to believe otherwise. I had taught English for thirty-one years and co-authored thirteen English textbooks. I took creative writing courses, even studying with renowned Canadian novelist Timothy Findley twice. Wasn't the transition to freelance writing a natural progression?

And it wasn't like I hadn't prepared myself for the end of my career. Retirement seminars were strongly recommended for educators. There were always rumours that teachers – especially those who taught English – could expect to live only two years after they left the classroom. Just in case we outlived those odds, Bonnie and I attended two evening retirement sessions.

The first session examined financial challenges we could expect to face. While some money specialists prophesy doom and gloom after retirement, others assure us we can retire on less than we think.[1] Bonnie and I were lucky not to have a mortgage, and our two daughters were grown with families of their own. We were down to one car. No more "work clothes" either. We had seniors' discounts to look forward to and, for once in our lives, the government would be taking less money in taxes.

I remember seeing a t-shirt touting "The one who dies with the most toys wins." It was quite the opposite in our house. We were constantly foisting off our stuff on friends and family.

The second seminar we attended focused more on what we were going to do post-retirement. We were given an exercise to start. "Describe your dream retirement. Don't hold back – anything you dream, put it down," the leader said. A buzz rose from the tables with occasional explosions of laughter as people fantasized with their partners or friends. Bonnie and I got to it. We had talked about this many times. First we wanted to win the lottery. Then anything became possible. We were ready.

$\sim$

Neither of my parents had a great retirement. My father was diagnosed with Parkinson's disease when he was around fifty and died just before his seventieth birthday. When he left his job, he couldn't drive, which meant he was home alone all day. He had so many falls, my mother quit her teaching job to stay home and care for him.

This forced retirement pushed my mother mentally and physically. My father garnered so much attention with his illness, my mother sort of faded into the background, dealing with day-to-day caretaking duties. I was not helpful, dropping in once a week, staying for an hour and leaving. (My sister, on the other hand, was a saint.) After my father's death, my mother's health declined. She had the means to have a good retirement but was in no shape to enjoy it. She spent the last ten years of her life wanting to die.

Watching my parents' non-retirement made me more determined to enjoy my own. My mother left us some money, which we invested in a tiny apartment in New Zealand. We had fallen in love with a small lakeside town on the South Island and the Canadian dollar was strong. Two years later, we found an affordable apartment in British Columbia's Okanagan Valley that we could rent out until we could move. Passionate skiers, we saw ourselves spending Canadian winters in the mountains, then travelling south to New Zealand for a second winter in the Southern Alps. For income, we'd rent out both places when we weren't there.

In the early 2000s, a story (probably apocryphal) circulated about a philosopher who, in her class, brought out a large glass jar. She filled it with small, round river stones. "Is it full?" she asked the students. They said yes. She then added gravel to the jar, shaking it so it settled between the stones.

"Is the jar full?" The students probably said no. They weren't going to be fooled twice. Next she poured sand into the jar, letting it filter through the gravel.

"Full?" Finally, she poured water into the jar until it came up to the brim.

"The stones," she said, "are the most important things in life. They have to go into the jar first. If you try to put them in at the end, it won't work."

We had places to live, and a plan, the stone foundations of our retirement.

I have always been on the top end of the Type A spectrum – not quite at the extreme, but definitely driven, obsessive and neurotic. While we taught, Bonnie and I tried for a work/life balance, but I wasn't overly successful. In the last fifteen years of my career, while teaching, I wrote textbooks. It took a huge time commitment to write, attend editorial meetings and revise while keeping up my marking and lesson preparation. But I loved it. It felt like important work – not more important than teaching, just different.

Bonnie had marking and lesson prep of her own. She also read voraciously, sometimes three books a week, and she painted.

Summers, I took writing workshops while Bonnie painted in our garden – beautiful, lush, brilliant oil paintings.

Singing was the one thing that gave us balance. We joined the LGBTQ choir Singing Out, and for fifteen years we spent Thursday nights at rehearsals. While we did this only one night a week, we spent hours learning music, memorizing words, even trying to master choralography.

It never failed that by Thursdays, Bonnie and I were exhausted. But singing is restorative. Inevitably, we came away from practice energized, our tense jaws, backs and necks relaxed from breathing deeply. Little in life beats singing beautiful harmonies, interpreting lyrics with the voice and laughing with eighty or so of your favourite people.

Moving west meant leaving the choir, the one thing I knew would create a hole in my life. I wasn't worried about making friends. I'm gregarious and extroverted. I had already planned on finding a yoga studio. We would meet people on the ski hill. The only drawback might be the size of the city. Was there an LGBTQ presence?

Bonnie retired six months before me. While I stayed with friends to complete my final semester in Ontario, she started reno-vating the apartment we had purchased in Kelowna. We Skyped every evening, catching up on the day's events. Bonnie walked me through the mess of renovations and showed me her art studio in the spare bedroom. She raved about her new painting group, and I regaled her with stories about world-famous bridges I was considering for a book I was writing. Terrified of heights, she felt nauseous just listening to me.

Skyping sometime in December, Bonnie couldn't wait to tell me about her latest adventure. She had driven out to a nearby winery to hear the Wyrd Sisters, a folk group from Winnipeg. I was surprised she went, since she doesn't like driving at night and the roads were snow covered. Arriving early (a chronic condition), she chatted up a couple seated with two other women at a nearby table. She eventually joined them. The two women pointed out a huge group sitting together. "They're all gay," they said.

Bonnie waved a list of phone numbers and emails in front of the camera. "Look. And we're going to keep in touch!"

As I sat in my little bedroom, surrounded by boxes ready for shipping, I had the oddest feeling. Bonnie had moved on without me. My head remained stuck in school, and she had slipped naturally into full retirement mode. Could I catch up?

The day after the fall term ended, I left for British Columbia.

The first nine months of retirement weren't an indicator of what "real" retirement looked like. I can't remember when I first saw the term "sugar rush" but that's what those first months were. We skied three times a week. Both Bonnie and I were now writing young adult non-fiction books, hers on art forgers, mine on tragic love stories. I even convinced her to collaborate on an idea I had for extreme vacations.

And that rush continued. We were living a fantasy life, someone else's life. At the end of ski season, we left on a to-hell-with-the-bell tour of the great European artworks Bonnie had taught for twenty-four years, but had never seen. This was the first time we had been able to travel outside school holidays. After two months driving through France, Holland and Italy, we flew to New Zealand for a second ski season.

Of course we couldn't continue to live like lottery winners. We started our "real" retirement when we returned to Canada in September. Bonnie painted at home or at the local arts centre with her artists' group. For sixteen years, I had been the one cloistered in my study after work and on weekends marking, preparing and writing. I hadn't noticed that Bonnie's art was also a solitary pursuit. She had filled her jar with stones and had made great strides with the gravel. I had stones in my jar; I needed to find some gravel. I joined a yoga class twice a week and began a regular walking routine to a local café where Bonnie had established a circle of coffee friends – retired people who arrived at the same time each day to hang out and chat. We discovered and befriended two gay men who had recently moved from Toronto and coincidently had used the same pierced and tattooed hairdresser as we had.

Our flurry of travel had allowed me to put off doing anything about my grand goal of becoming a freelance writer, and psychologically, establishing my identity as a retired person was proving harder than I had imagined.

While working, I couldn't understand teachers whose jobs defined them. Suddenly I wondered if I was one of them. I was no longer a teacher. My book-writing career had come to an end. Even in retirement, Bonnie was still an artist. What was I?

In *Revitalizing Retirement,* Nancy Schlossberg says, "retirement challenges your identity, your relationships and may leave you feeling rootless if you have no purpose."[2] I felt rootless. Most of my friends back east were still teaching. Our new friends were happily retired. One, a wine connoisseur, worked part time in a winery. Another, coming from the fashion industry, did some consulting with a condominium developer, choosing finishes and colours. Others volunteered.

I said when I retired I was going to be a writer. Having taught literature (say that with a slightly snooty fake English accent) for thirty-one years, and studied writing, I had internalized the damaging message that writers are exalted beings. I've never forgotten the story of the famous Canadian novelist, Margaret Laurence, meeting a brain surgeon at a cocktail party. When he told her he was going to be a writer when he retired, apparently she responded, "What a coincidence! When I retire, I'm going to be a brain surgeon."

The point, as I eventually learned, is that writing, like everything else, is less a gift than a choice —a choice to work very hard at becoming…something. Pablo Picasso didn't become a Cubist because he couldn't draw. He spent years studying and practicing. Like the brain surgeon, I thought because of my other experience, I could skip that part.

I felt I had to prove I belonged in the writers' community. But, embarrassingly, instead of sitting down and writing, dealing with rejection, learning from mistakes and getting better, I prepared and sent applications for memberships in two professional writing associations. Based on the volume of my educational writing, I was accepted by the Writers' Union of Canada and the Canadian Authors' Association, giving me that much needed "writer" label. But as a popular Facebook meme so aptly points out, "Standing in a garage doesn't make you a car."

I came across an ad for columnists in the Sunday edition of the local Okanagan newspaper. It started: "Calling all writers…" In a moment of optimism (fuelled, no doubt by my new membership cards) I thought, "I can do that." I copied the editor's name and email address. My first piece, on the popularity of coffee shops, is still framed on my study wall and with it, a note saying, "Thanks for the coffee. Love the column and would like to publish it." Three more columns followed. I pitched some ideas to *Okanagan Life* magazine. While in each case the editor asked for a different approach, all three feature articles were published. A local arts magazine took two more pieces.

Through a friend's introduction, I started writing the occasional advertorial (an advertisement that reads like an article) for a local food and wine magazine. I joined winemakers and owners in pre-sales tastings, sat with a cheesemaker learning about matching specific cheeses with wine, and interviewed top chefs. Even though I spent far more than my pay cheque on Okanagan wine and gourmet meals, I loved this job. It was perfect for a retired person. I was doing it. My jar quickly filled with gravel.

I plucked up the nerve to pitch a monthly column to the paper, in which I would profile an interesting local. To my surprise, the editor liked it. I found and interviewed three people to start: a twenty-two-year-old former skateboard champion who suffered a heart attack at nineteen that left him with brain damage; an entrepreneur who inadvertently became involved with the Russian mafia when he started a science and tech business in Russia; and an eighteen-year-old aspiring opera singer.

I was loving retirement, or my interpretation of it. I really thought I had it all worked out. Then my contract arrived in the mail. The paper would hold the rights to all my work. I didn't know anything about copyright, less about newspapers. I hadn't paid much attention to my textbook contracts. But time and again in fiction-writing workshops, I had heard, "Don't give away your copyright." I approached the paper to see if I could change the wording. Not possible. I turned down the offer. I thought I was doing the right thing. If I were given the same opportunity today, I would take it.

A host of rejections followed. My early successes had filled me with false confidence. It's easy to see now that I was like every newly minted graduate. I was starting on a new career, and although I knew how to write, I had little practical experience. I saw every rejection as a criticism of my ability. I didn't consider that the timing of my submissions might have been off, that my pitches had been poorly worded or that my ideas may not have been the best fit for the magazines I was pitching. After thirty-one years teaching and sixteen years in educational writing I was back at ground zero, a novice.

I recently listened to a 2017 interview on CBC where Willem Dafoe talked about being involved in what he calls "a task" or "a structure" and the positive impact that can have on the way we deal with feeling insignificant in this world. When he's part of a structure (whether it's acting in a play or in a movie), he feels like he's at the centre, like he's connected to everything. "Our whole life is haunted by validation, trying to feel like we are someone and finding identity... But if you feel connected, feel at the centre of things, you don't worry about that." By being at the centre of things, he says, people feel freer, stronger, even more creative.

Suddenly I found myself shoved to the periphery of my own retirement. I had lost my centre. When I studied psychology in university, one of the first things we learned in Psych 101 was Maslow's hierarchy of basic needs: physical needs (food, water, air, sleep); the need for security (safety, shelter, stability); social needs (belonging, love, inclusion); the need for self-esteem (power, recognition, prestige); self-actualization (the need for development, creativity, problem solving). Not until I started reflecting on how retirement deskilled me, made me feel almost powerless and excluded, did I think of that hierarchy as anything but fixed. I always thought one moved up through the needs as one aged and matured. But now I see it's like a sieve, or more accurately, like a pasta strainer with very large holes. Wherever I go, I see panhandlers on the street. Are they homeless? Who can say? But if given a choice, most would probably not be standing on a corner begging for change in -20°, dealing with the most basic physiological and safety needs. That doesn't mean they haven't been at the top of the pyramid with good jobs, safe homes and loving families.

While I knew I was loved unconditionally, when it came to belonging and self-esteem, I felt like I was standing on the edge of a swimming pool and some smartass kept grabbing my shoulders, pretending to push me in, only to pull me back at the last minute.

One thing I lacked was resilience. Maybe that's an age thing. We get too secure in our structures and routines and, like our aging skin, lose elasticity. My ego had definitely taken a knock. "You don't have what it takes to be a writer," my external validator hissed. Looking back, by the time we arrived in Paris this fear had burrowed parasitically into my brain.

What I didn't know was that I was not alone. In a study conducted across sixteen European countries and the United States, Dr. Elizabeth Mokyr Horner found many retirees experience a high immediately after retirement as they fulfill their dreams of golfing, travelling, even sitting around doing nothing. A few years later, however, a crash and a decline in happiness follows the rush.[3] I wish I had read Mokyr Horner at the time. I might have recognized the rush/crash cycle.

Recently, Bonnie observed that I rarely do anything entirely alone. She is an only child. When she was ten, her father was diagnosed with multiple sclerosis. She didn't have birthday parties, sleepovers, or anything rowdy that could disturb her father or her mother, who had become the main earner and caregiver. Growing up in a small town, Bonnie spent hours playing by herself and, as she got older, she spent her time skiing, reading and lifeguarding, all solitary activities. She is happy in her own company, which is why being an artist suits her personality. While she makes friends easily, she doesn't need those friends around her all the time. She hates group work. What she does love is working alongside other artists when everyone is occupied with their own personal goals. It's the adult equivalent of parallel play.

I grew up with siblings. I enjoy group activities. While I love research and the solitary nature of creating, I like to talk about writing, mine and others'.

When we were still employed, the differences in our personalities were never an issue. We used to joke about being happily codependent, but in retirement, that wasn't working. One of the many people who writes about retirement, Ernie Zelinsky (*How to Retire Happy, Wild and Free*), says to handle the freedom of retirement we need to become highly independent and have confidence in our ability to live life without depending on anyone else. The less I wrote, the less confident I felt, and the more I wanted to spend time with Bonnie. I'd wander into her studio: "Want to go to the mall with me?" Occasionally, she'd acquiesce. More often, she didn't.

I lost interest in finding stories. The gravel in my jar was on the verge of spilling out.

As I walked out to meet friends for coffee one morning, I gave myself a stern lecture. "Look around. No one else is having trouble with retirement. Stop your moaning. Get a life." I was listening to Singing Out on my iPod at the time. That's what was missing – a choir. What about a church choir? No. Sitting through Sunday services was out of the question. Were there choirs that accepted new members mid-season? No. The only alternative was to put an ad in the local paper and on an LGBTQ site, seeking singers for a gay choir. Within weeks, eight brave men and women gathered around the piano in our living room to decide whether or not we could create a chorus. We had people come from up and down the Okanagan

Valley. We didn't have a director (and I have no skills in that area), but we had some enthusiasm and some music and within two weeks we had a new member, John, a pianist and music therapist who led us through our weekly practices. Sometimes there were only three people besides Bonnie and me. Sometimes we had ten. We called ourselves The Okanagan Fruit Company.

I tried to find a director. I wrote to every gay or LBGTQ chorus I could think of asking if they knew anyone in our area who might be interested. A few months later, the director of the Vancouver Gay Men's chorus emailed me. He didn't know anyone, but his chorus was coming to town and wondered if we would like to perform one of our own songs and then join his group on another. He would send us the music. This was huge. When I approached our choir, one woman said she couldn't sing in public for fear of losing her job. The rest agreed.

Ironically, Bonnie and I wouldn't be in town that weekend, which threatened the feasibility of performing. I brazenly asked a group of women singers who belonged to the local church to join us. The Anglican church was not that gay friendly, but to my delight, these women were open and accepting and they agreed. At the concert, one forward-thinking member put out a signup sheet and we got a few more recruits for the fall.

We found a director – a music teacher who taught in the local middle school – and when an LGBTQ centre opened over the summer, their board sought groups to sponsor. We were given the centre rent-free for rehearsals and money to help pay for music and the director. John became the accompanist and recorded each part instrumentally for those who didn't read music. In May and June the following year, we performed two concerts in each of two cities, our own and Penticton. We sold out all four shows. I was so proud of our little group. I was once again at the centre and connected.

When Bonnie and I headed for New Zealand that summer, our chorus had a constitution, a board, a fall rehearsal schedule and music on order. I happily spent hours sitting at the dining table, learning GarageBand (the Apple recording program), then singing individual parts into the computer. After posting the completed

CDs back to Canada, I felt a certain almost-smug sense of satisfaction thinking about how much easier it would be for the singers to learn their parts in the fall. Come September, we joined the group for rehearsals via Skype. Sand sifted and filtered through my jar, filling the spaces between the gravel.

And then someone drilled a hole in the bottom.

The choir fell apart, badly and soul crushingly. While in New Zealand, I got emails from one member, then another about how they felt left out or unheard. One woman, a close friend, quit over a dispute she and her partner were having outside the choir with another member. When one of the original group overheard a comment about his inability to hold a tune, he too quit. Then the director turned in her notice.

The choir disbanded. While Bonnie was invested in the chorus, she didn't own it like I did. She never joined the board, and she didn't really like memorizing lyrics. Recently she admitted that the time she had to spend on the choir was a distraction from her art. She felt sorrier for me than for the group's expiration. I, on the other hand, felt like someone ran over my dog and left his corpse on the road right in front of my house.

I tried joining a book group and attended the local Authors Association meetings, but couldn't find my niche.

Travel took the pressure off. We made two more trips overseas. I had Bonnie's undivided attention twenty-four hours a day and everything was new, from landscapes to art galleries to museums. But travel is temporary, like fugitive colour in a painting.

"What is this woman complaining about? It all sounds perfect. I wish I could have her life." Go ahead. Say it. I heard that all the time, which made me feel more of a fraud, more guilty for not being grateful, convinced there was something seriously wrong with me. That is the insidious part of a retirement that looks perfect from the outside but doesn't feel that way inside. I probably should have gotten some help, looking back on it now.

A couple of years ago, I was in Toronto researching a painting that hangs in Sunnybrook Health Centre. My sister-in-law drove me to my appointment. She retired just before me and she and my brother travel extensively. As we chatted about their many trips, she said, "The travel is great; it's the in-between times that are difficult." Difficult? How was that possible? They had the perfect retirement. But I was relieved to hear it.

People in my family don't talk about problems; I was brought up in a "stiff upper lip" household. My father couldn't deal with emotion. When my best friend, Maureen, moved from Toronto to Winnipeg at the end of sixth grade, I was inconsolable. "Stop your blathering," my father yelled. According to him, there wasn't anything I could do, there would be other friends and I was a blithering idiot. My mother suggested I cry in my room instead of draping myself over the back of the couch staring out the front window.

My grandfather committed suicide when my mother was twelve. That was no secret. But my mother was eighty, hospitalized and sedated before she finally told me that she had found her father's body in the garage where he had gassed himself. She tried to kill herself at least once (that I know of) before she finally starved herself to death in a nursing home at the age of eighty-three. How might her life have been different if she had told us earlier? Secrets held close, never shared, hurt those who keep them and those who never know them.

I kept my feelings hidden. What right did a woman so privileged, so fortunate, have to be dissatisfied? My solution was to pretend. Look fulfilled. Look busy. I crammed my days with distractions – yoga twice a week in the studio as well as at least two other mornings of home practice. When we weren't skiing (a welcomed group activity), I walked five or more kilometres "to stay in shape." I stopped reading and started watching hours of television, mindless programs on house hunting and entertainment, as well as *NCIS* and *CSI* reruns. Sometimes I'd spend four to five hours a day in front of the set. I'd also escape into sleep, taking afternoon naps, in bed by eight. I could claim to anyone who asked that I was so busy, I didn't know where the hours went.

Meanwhile, Bonnie's life exploded with colour. She painted and sketched and drew *en plein air* with her art group. Landscapes, portraits, watercolours, oils. And then she was accepted into the course in Paris.

At first, I thought "Perfect. Travel always makes me feel good." I researched places I could visit while Bonnie was in school. But I had this persistent Greek chorus in my brain. "You can't do it," it whispered over and over. I could have shut out that voice had it not been amplified by my realization that for this trip, I would be alone five days a week. I had never toured by myself, and I have an abysmal sense of direction and an irrational fear of getting lost. Although I boasted I would be a *flâneuse,* I couldn't picture myself finding my way around a city I didn't know, where my lack of confidence to speak French limited any kind of meaningful interaction with others.

I kept my anxiety in check, making lists – clothing and shoes I would need to buy and pack, recipes I could make, groceries we'd have to buy – searching endlessly online for accommodation and figuring out flight routes and times. I poured over tour books and maps and researched different areas of the city. At night, I'd wake up with that Greek chorus screaming, "What hasn't been said about Paris? What can *you* find that hasn't been discovered by thousands already?"

But January came, and we were in Paris.

∿

Day one, Bonnie needed art supplies. We walked along cobble-stoned streets and descended five flights of stairs. With her bat-like sonar, she steered us down one street, then another, to Adam's Art Supplies. It was closed for lunch.

We found a little café nearby, crowded with locals, who greeted each other with double kisses as they came through the door. What could be more French, more Parisian? I started to relax.

As we headed back to the art store after lunch, two young teen-agers, who must have heard us speaking English as they followed us, walked by and in unison shouted, "Suck my dick." I hadn't heard language like that since my days checking out the smoking pit at school. I may not have known where I was, but I knew these kids. I flipped them the bird. I could handle this.

On my own for the first time the next day, I arranged to meet Bonnie at the Louvre Museum so we could travel back home together. I didn't know how to use the métro and the museum stood three kilometres from our apartment, in a mostly straight line. How difficult could it be? I spent a good part of the morning moving between the toilet and the dining table, where I wrote out directions in a small notebook. I had convinced myself that consulting a notebook was far less conspicuous than struggling with an unwieldy map. If I looked less like a tourist, maybe I'd avoid pickpockets and scam artists. The fact that I wore running shoes, outdoor pants from Mountain Equipment Co-op, and earmuffs might have given me away. Just before I walked out the door, I tucked my *MapGuide* inside the notebook, in case I needed to double-check directions.

I cursed Baron Haussmann for the uniform appearance of classical Paris. Every avenue and boulevard looked the same to me. The street I followed changed names five times – rue des Martyrs, rue Fléchier, rue Lafitte, rue de Gramont, rue Sainte Anne – and shifted slightly to the right or left as it did. Did I wonder who was martyred there, where the arrowmaker might have lived, who M. Laffitte might have been and what Sainte Anne was famous for? Unlike the *flâneur,* that inquisitive, carefree, strolling fellow from the early twentieth century, I marched like a Roman conqueror, with a schedule, route and strategic battle plan. Woe betide anyone or anything that got in my way. For three kilometres, I raised my eyes from my notebook just long enough to check that I was still on the right street. By the time I reached the Louvre, I was mentally exhausted.

Here I was, six years into retirement in one of the most romantic cities in the world. I had to make this work. But I needed some serious help.

I found it in an unusual guise – a dead French pop singer.

CHAPTER 2

THE DEAD SINGER NEXT DOOR: NOTICING WHAT'S RIGHT BESIDE YOU

"What the…?" I pulled open our living room window and leaned out over the wrought-iron grill to see a tourist group gathered directly below me. A single female voice speaking Italian said "*Something, something, something,* Dalida, *something…tràgico.*" And then again, "Dalida." At the end of her spiel, various group members took photos of the stone wall running 90° to our building.

About an hour later, a second group – Asian this time – listened to their guide, then took photos of the wall, selfies pointing to the wall, and photos of each other in front of the wall. When a French group stopped within another fifteen minutes, I had to know.

Rue d'Orchampt is a tiny cobblestone street in Montmartre. From place Émile Goudeau, it runs 145 metres in a dogleg to rue Lepic. Our apartment on rue d'Orchampt lay equal steps from the Bateau-Lavoir where Picasso painted his breakthrough Cubist work, *Desmoiselles d'Avignon,* and the iconic windmill in Pierre-Auguste Renoir's *Bal du Moulin de la Galette.*

Living in such a legendary neighbourhood, I expected to hear tourists on the street outside. But what intrigued them about a stone wall?

I went down the stairs to the street. A plaque, about 100×50 cm., read "*Dalida a vécu dans cette maison de 1962 à 1987. Ses amis Monmartrois ne l'oblieront pas,*" which translates as "Dalida lived in this house from 1962 to 1987. Her Montmartre friends will not forget her."

Who the hell was Dalida (pronounced, I learned, with the accent on the first and last syllables) that she attracted so much attention?

The first page of my Google search listed her official website, a Wikipedia entry (of course) and hundreds of photographs. In early pictures, her hair is long and brunette and backcombed. Her eyebrows, dark and accentuated with eyebrow pencil, complement the black-lined eyes – very Sophia Loren. As the years pass, her hair lightens, her fifties shirtwaist dresses become long flowing gowns, and by the disco era she's got big hair and wears head-to-toe metallic glam dresses slit to the hip.

I found page after page of YouTube performances and news articles, discovering as I delved further into her life that she was one of France's most famous singing stars, on par with Edith Piaf and Charles Aznavour. No wonder her house attracted tourists.

At only fifty-four, Dalida committed suicide in the house behind the gated stone wall, the house next door on rue d'Orchampt. Her suicide note read, "Life is unbearable, please forgive me."[1] The tour guide was right; it was *tràgico*.

I clicked on television footage of her funeral. Coverage started with shots of our street, the large gate into her yard and, because her garden wall abutted the façade of our apartment, the windows of our salon. Four liveried men carried the black-and-white draped casket from her house to the street and slid it into the hearse. Mourners stood silently on rue d'Orchampt. Many wept.

The impression I got from all the photos and videos was that this woman had it all – and yet, she wasn't happy. I had it all. I was in Paris. But I was forcing myself to get up and get out of the house.

In a city famous for its museums, the Eiffel Tower, the Grands Boulevards and shopping, it is ironic that a story of a woman I had never heard of enticed me beyond the confines of my three-kilometre path to the Louvre. She was buried in Cimetière de Montmartre (Montmartre Cemetery). I'd seen it from the #95 bus when Bonnie and I returned from the museum. I got out my *MapGuide*. Only six blocks.

Getting lost. It's one of those irrational fears I have, probably stemming from some childhood trauma. I do recall walking down a busy street with my parents and suddenly finding myself trying to hold hands with a stranger wearing the same coat as my mother. I remember the panic I felt when I looked into that stranger's eyes.

But I won't use a GPS when I'm walking. I'm too cheap to pay data costs and besides I don't really know how to use the GPS on my phone. I prefer a paper map. Really, I'm only making excuses because I'm a luddite. But here's a good reason I recently discovered to use a map. It's the answer I'm going to give any time anyone asks me why I'm not using my GPS. According to neuroscientists, we have three types of neurons to help us navigate: place cells (individual neurons that fire in an individual place, which together create a cognitive map); grid cells, which act like "You are here" pins, noting important locations"[2]: and head direction cells, which fire when we face north, south, east and west. All these cells are located in the hippocampus, the place where memories are formed. When we use the GPS on our devices, we create less accurate maps in our heads than when we use a traditional map or when we figure out where we are by getting lost and finding our way. By using a GPS, we can almost turn off our memory centre, and many studies have linked the shrinking of the hippocampus with an increased risk of dementia.[3] Lecture complete.

Neuroscientists suggest using our brains instead of a GPS could improve how well our hippocampus works and might help delay cognitive decline as we age. It takes more effort to form cognitive maps, but if keeping the hippocampus active means staving off the inevitable, I'll continue using a traditional map.[4]

There's something else about using a map. I started highlighting where I'd been. When I unfolded that map each day and copied directions into my notebook, all those bright orange lines were something immediately visual, physical evidence of existence. Maybe because I felt so invisible, so adrift, the map was proof I was still there.

~

It was after two in the afternoon by the time I headed down to rue des Abbesses, which, according to my map, should have led me to the entrance of Montmartre Cemetery. Sure enough, the large green metal gates to the cemetery were exactly where my notes said they would be. But they were closed. I looked for a handle, peered through the keyhole, pushed with all my strength. The gates didn't budge. I had a growing sense of cognitive dissonance.

Cemeteries in Toronto are generally surrounded by fences, which are easy to jump or scale, even after hours. As a teenager I spent the occasional Saturday night hanging out amongst the granite headstones at the local graveyard, smoking cigarettes and drinking from a wineskin. I assumed French cemeteries would be similar. But this gate and the three-metre-high stone walls made me doubt myself. Maybe the cemetery was closed. But why would a cemetery be closed in the middle of the day? Much later, I discovered those large gates open one day a year, la Toussaint, the day the French honour their dead.

Turning left, tracing the bus route across the bridge spanning the graveyard below, I couldn't see another way in, and I refused to jettison myself over the railing. By the time I made it to the next major street, I'd run out of cemetery. What I didn't see then – which now is so evident – was a set of stairs descending from the bridge to the main entrance. Defeated, I turned toward home. I was pissed off, angry at myself for not being able to find the entrance, and angry at Paris for taunting me with its giant cemetery but keeping its entrance secret. My nose must have been momentarily out of my notebook, or I would have missed the small sign at the corner of avenue Rachel pointing to the cemetery. Like the stairs from the bridge, this entrance became obvious once I knew about it and later in the trip I frequently divulged its location to other lost tourists.

It had started to rain, and the January dusk seemed earlier than usual. Inside the gates, a permanent map listed the whereabouts of the most sought-after graves. I tried to imprint the way to the Eighteenth Division, where I would find Dalida, but unless I took time to write detailed instructions, my cognitive mapmaking skills were still weak at best. I made a lame attempt —up some stairs, along a narrow beaten path covered with moldering fall leaves. I didn't know when cemeteries closed in Paris, but I had seen those giant green gates. I didn't want to be the Canadian senior who French police had to rescue from the locked graveyard.

But I also refused to let a bunch of dead people defeat me. Cemetery plans were available; I had seen people using them. That evening, I looked at the cemetery guide online and returned the next day determined to get a map and find Dalida.

Montmartre Cemetery belies its name. While it is situated on the hill, its eleven-hectare site originated below street level in an open pit mine. Before its official opening in 1825, abandoned tunnels were used as ad hoc burial grounds; according to Paris's Convention and Visitor's Bureau website, one mine served as a mass grave for 700 Swiss Guards who died defending the Tuileries in August 1792.[5]

As I walked down rue des Abbesses, I practiced two sentences I had looked up the night before. "*Excusez-moi de vous déranger. Avez-vous un plan du cimetière?*" (Excuse me for interrupting. Do you have a map of the cemetery?)

Inside the cemetery gates, a small building on the right, a bookstore or museum, looked like it might have a map. My heart thumped, I took a deep breath, rehearsed the question one last time and tried the handle. It didn't move.

On the left stood a guardhouse of sorts. I had anticipated speaking to a salesperson or a tourist representative behind a large desk or counter, not a handsome, Black, nail-bejewelled *gardienne* in a small, intimate space. I stood outside the door, not quite pressing my nose against the pane of glass, until she motioned me in.

Excited and nervous, I blurted out, "Do you speak English? I'm looking for *un plan du cimetière*."

She didn't answer right away, but drilled a look straight through me and in elegantly French-accented English said, "Can't you say *bonjour*?" My internal furnace exploded, flushing sweat through every pore of my body. How rude I sounded without any sort of greeting, launching into what *I* wanted in *my* language.

"*Désolé.*" I said, bowing slightly from the waist, my hands in a sort of *namaste* position to acknowledge my faux pas. It didn't feel adequate. I used *désolé* when I accidently tromped on someone's foot, unwittingly butted into line, or inadvertently brushed someone on the street. It was a quick reaction to an embarrassing situation, a version of the Canadian "sorry." But that day I felt truly humbled. The attendant smiled. "*Bon. Qu'est-ce que vous désirez?*" (Good. What would you like?) I had been told. It was over – at least in her head.

I walked about sixty steps further into the cemetery, clutching my map, stopping under the noisy, unattractive metal thoroughfare, still feeling the sting of humiliation. One inner voice repeated: *Breathe in, breathe out.* A second scolded: *Get over yourself. You're acting like a child.*

I admit I overreact to many things. Bonnie loves to describe how upset I was on receiving our first joint Visa bill. She was shocked. "Did we spend that money? Did we enjoy the things we bought?" she asked. Of course, she was right.

I improved over the years, but my increased feelings of insecurity about who I was and what I was going do in my retirement set me back. I think if, before going to Paris, I had read Oliver Burkeman's *The Antidote: Happiness for People Who Can't Stand Positive Thinking*, I might have dealt with the cemetery guard incident much more calmly, more rationally. In Burkeman's book, he takes on an exercise designed by a psychologist who helped his patients overcome anxiety. The psychologist, Albert Ellis, assigned his patients deliberately humiliating tasks to perform in public – tasks that weren't dangerous, lewd or against the law – to demonstrate how irrationally they approached even slightly unpleasant experiences.

Ellis was a self-avowed Stoic who described stoicism as "developing a muscular calm in the face of trying circumstances."[6] I love that term: "muscular calm." It's so hard and soft at the same time, invoking images of fighting and passivity all at once. Ellis believed that when we put ourselves in humiliating situations we face our feelings about embarrassment and quickly understand that our fears about what *might* happen don't match what actually *does* happen.

Burkeman, who admits he's never handled embarrassment well, decided to try "the subway station experiment." While riding the London subway, he loudly announced each station before the automated voice. At first, he was embarrassed. Then he noticed that no one really paid attention to him. No one got angry. No one tried to attack him. He realized he had been worried that people might think badly about him. And there it is – the need for external validation (or in this case the fear of losing that validation). That describes me. My need to get a membership card that says I'm a writer. My need for others to think I'm OK.

It's easy to look back on my faux pas with the *gardienne* and see how the situation actually pushed me forward. I couldn't articulate it then, but the humiliation was mixed with some relief – nothing tragic happened. No one died. I doubt she remembered the encounter an hour after it happened. And I learned something valuable about French manners – always say "*bonjour*" – a lesson that stood me in good stead every day.

Stoics believe anxiety stems from how we view an experience. I saw my faltering attempts at reconfiguring my retirement as failures. And I convinced myself others saw me the same way. Burkeman suggests that to be happy one has to examine how things could go wrong. "Confronting the worst case scenario saps it of its anxiety-producing power."[7] I understand the concept, but if I had imagined the worst-case scenario in retirement – retirement being the sum of its parts, an amorphous blob, an event – would I have been afraid to try anything in fear that it could fail? Maybe when it comes to post-work life we should examine the various things we want to do individually. What might happen if injuries prevented me from going to yoga – what could I do instead? If I could no longer ski, how would that affect my relationship with winter? If no one wants to publish my work, what are some other avenues I could follow? If I'd imagined, before I retired, a Plan B, and maybe C, D and E, I might have been able to manage the setbacks more successfully.

~

I studied my cemetery map, double-checking the names of each street (Paris cemeteries are criss-crossed by *chemins* and *avenues*) and started down a major avenue I thought would take me to the pop singer's grave. Having missed the most direct route (so typical), I found myself at the end of avenue Hector Berlioz staring into an underpass stacked with wheelbarrows and tools. The plan showed a through street, but it looked like a dead end to me. Here I was imagining the worst-case scenario. I could see the headlines in the Canadian press: "Retired School Teacher Attacked and Left for Dead in Paris Cemetery." I held my breath, walked as quickly as possible and emerged on the other side. The worst hadn't happened. And there it was – chemin des Gardes, the street where Dalida lay. Such a small victory; such an immense relief.

In a graveyard filled with sepulchres the size of phone booths large enough for someone to enter, kneel and pray, and extravagant monuments boasting classical sculptures in granite or bronze, Dalida's monument is overwhelmingly modern. "Glitzy" might be a better description. She stands, life-sized, sculpted in white marble, dressed in a spaghetti-strapped gown. Her hands are by her side, her chin slightly raised, eyes closed. She steps onto the stage for her final performance. Behind her head, rays emanate from a halo superimposed on a black marble backdrop like the Virgin Mary surrounded by a proscenium arch.

Fresh bouquets and floral arrangements – tributes from fans – lined the front of her grave. I couldn't take my eyes off her. Five or six people stopped. Some left flowers. One left a stone at her feet. Dalida died in 1987. These fans spanned all age groups. I felt like part of a secret society, relieved that my fascination with this woman was not unique. We definitely needed a sign or symbol, something like St. James's scallop shell, which identifies pilgrims on their way to Santiago de Compostela. Perhaps a filmy white scarf draped artfully across the neck and over the shoulders.

I couldn't wait for Bonnie to get home to show her pictures of the grave. Admittedly, Dalida became an obsession. I watched her performances online; during Skype conversations, I'd lean out the window with my computer, so friends and family could hear tour guides tell Dalida's story in the language of the moment. About three blocks from our apartment, I found place Dalida, which features a bronze bust of the singer, breasts polished by many hands.

I knew she was having some weird effect on me when, sitting at the dining table, my back to the window, chatting with our daughter on Skype, D'arcy looked over my shoulder and asked, "Who's looking in the window?"

"There can't be anyone looking in the window. We're on the second floor."

"There's someone looking in the window. I can see a face."

I turned to look. The external shutters were closed. "No one there."

"I'm taking a screen shot. There's someone behind the curtains." She sent me the shot. Through the folds of the sheers, pressed an unmistakable face, small, female, eerily like the face of Dalida's grave sculpture. No word of a lie.

Over those nine weeks in Paris, I spent hours in art galleries surrounded by gold, vermillion, orange, yellow and blue, but Dalida – dead as she was – created a palette of spectacular possibilities, a story to pursue, a life to examine.

~

People kill themselves for many reasons. Whatever the cause, they see continuing to live as a less viable option than death. As a teenager, I often had thoughts of suicide, although I never acted on them. My grandfather asphyxiated himself in his garage, a victim of the Great Depression, and my mother tried pills at least once before she opted to starve herself in the end. I know if I get an incurable disease, I will request an assisted suicide.

From the outside, Dalida seemed to have everything going for her. But as I dug deeper, I found a life in conflict. On the eve of her engagement to Luigi Tenco, a singer/songwriter who Dalida worked and performed with, Tenco shot and killed himself after he lost a song-writing competition.[8] Dalida attempted suicide shortly thereafter. Lucienne Morisse, her first husband and former manager, stayed by Dalida's side throughout her recovery. *He* committed suicide three years later. A third lover, Richard Chanfray, with whom she had lived for nine years, committed suicide two years after their split.

Did she feel responsible? Was she terrified every time she fell in love?

I've never worried that my relationship with Bonnie would end – except in death. When our nine weeks in Paris finished, Bonnie suggested they were a preparation for our ultimate separation, assuming – of course, she would go first. While the suggestion upset me – it sounded like I was making deliberate, calculated steps towards that end – in a way she was right. I was forced to make a move toward independence I never would have taken at home in Canada.

∼

Two weeks after arriving on rue d'Orchampt, while sitting at breakfast, I heard an operatic voice, unrestrained and mostly on key. I opened the window and peered out. The street lights still glowed. Remnants of a previous snowfall clung to the edges where the buildings met the sidewalks. A man, maybe in his thirties, in a red beret and scarf, walked toward Dalida's mansion singing one of her early hits, "Bambino." He sang with joy, without a hint of self-consciousness.

Several times a week, always before sunrise, he strolled down our street, singing a Dalida song. Unlike those who wanted to sleep, I looked forward to his performances. He must have known Dalida's entire repertoire.

If the morning singer had ever seen Dalida alive, he'd have been very young. "Bambino" topped the charts in 1956, the year *I* turned four. If the young man was thirty, he would have been four when she died.

A third generation still sang her songs.

How do we mere mortals know what we've left behind? I always hoped that something I did in the classroom or in the hallways or even in the swimming pool (I coached the swim team) had a positive impact on a student. Bonnie claims my textbooks influenced a generation of students. I remember exactly one textbook from high school – *Living Latin* – and only because Lenny Lombardi cut out its centre to conceal his squirt gun.

Textbooks are important to teachers. When my writing partners and I started to put together the textbooks we wrote, we tried to figure out what teachers needed most. How could we write a book that helped teachers deal with mixed-ability classes? How could we build in the increased demand for media literacy? What could we do to help teachers address special needs? I remember fighting to include a story with a gay character – probably the first in a high school anthology. Of course, publishers need to sell texts and we were warned against controversial topics, especially if they might scare off non-secular school boards. I'd like to think that our texts helped teachers.

If I did leave something to the students I taught, I'm damn sure it wasn't in a textbook. It would have been in an assignment or in a lesson or in a private chat. And when students do get in touch, their words are precious. No longer living where I taught, getting together with teacher friends, taking part in reunions or even attending funerals is difficult. Six years into retirement, I feared fading away, leaving nothing behind. My mother once pointed out that, after a certain age, we are ignored. As she got older, and as my siblings and I married and had children, we left my mother out of conversations at family dinners. *We* were the ones still working, raising children, creating new lives for ourselves. *We* had important things to talk about. My mother's retired life seemed inconsequential compared to ours. And here I was feeling the same way she did.

～

It became commonplace to find tourists huddled around the dedication plaque or trying to peer over the wall at Dalida's fairy-tale mansion (which by this time had been divided up and sold as million-dollar condos.) My third week in Paris, I rounded the dogleg to see an older man standing on the sidewalk staring at Dalida's house. He wore a long overcoat, a scarf and a winter fedora. I couldn't help but walk in front of him as I crossed the street to our door. *"Pardon,"* I said. When I looked at him, he was crying. Did he take a date to Dalida's concert? Dance to her music in a club, a disco ball spinning overhead?

Music is like the *Star Trek* transporter. When I hear "Happy Together" by the Turtles, I'm instantly beamed into a blue Volkswagen beetle with my eighteen-year-old boyfriend on a sunny, spring day crossing the Humber River on the Queen Elizabeth Way in Toronto. In 2012, Music and Memory, a non-profit organization, made a documentary on its project to purchase iPods for use in care homes. One part of that video went viral – the story of Henry, a patient who had been in care for ten years. Uncommunicative, Henry was given an iPod with music selected specifically for him based on recommendations from his caregiver and his daughter. The philosopher, Immanuel Kant, called music "the quickening art," and that's what happened to Henry. He bounced and hummed, and afterwards, when asked questions by the doctor, could answer in complete sentences and sing entire verses of "I'll Be Home for Christmas," things he had been unable to do before.[10]

Music also connects us.

The man in the red beret sang Dalida's music, and the old man in the overcoat relived some memory through her songs. When I saw the old man standing on our corner, I had a flash of my father. He loved music. When we were young, he'd sit at the piano and play us to bed, always with the same two pieces: "The Darktown Strutter's Ball" and "Alexander's Ragtime Band." He never had a piano lesson in his life, and he couldn't read music. He played by ear in the key of C, so he only occasionally had to hit the pesky black notes. My father has been dead over twenty years. He may not have won any prizes.

He may not have been written up in books. But he left me something as important as Dalida's gift to the world: my musical ear.

At that moment, I longed to sit down and play those songs the way he had.

My piano had become a piece of furniture. Like many people, when I first retired, I planned to play each day. That didn't happen. Living on the top floor of our apartment building, our piano could be heard in the apartments below and in the hallway. While I took lessons as a child, I hated to practice and, because I have a good ear, I'm a terrible sight reader. I listened to my teachers play and tried to remember how the pieces sounded instead of reading the notes. I play badly (I never play in public), and knowing others could hear all my mistakes embarrassed me. I stopped playing altogether.

Reading about Dalida, listening to her music, hearing the young man singing her songs and seeing the old man weeping on the street in front of her house reminded me of the importance of music in my life – strumming guitar around a campfire, playing and singing folk music in school talent shows with my friend, the high school band, Singing Out, The Okanagan Fruit Company.

When we returned from Paris, I traded in our piano for an electronic model so I could play with earphones. I would be lying if I said I practise every day, but I play more often. And I try to learn new pieces. I can bang away at any hour of the day and no one can hear me.

I pick up my guitar more often as well. Sometimes I'll sing for two hours at a time. Sadly, the lyrics of those '60s protest songs ring true even today.

A 2010 literature review conducted by Lisa J. Lehmberg and C. Victor Fung showed seniors who play an instrument feel healthier and less stressed.[11] I get that. Breathing deeply and exercising the diaphragm are great for relaxation and health, and playing piano and finger picking on the guitar take dexterity, something we lose with age if we don't practise. While making music at home has become an important part of my revitalization, I still yearn for a group to sing with. This is partly for the challenge of learning new music but also for the social aspect of a choral environment, first working together in my section to get the notes right, then working with other sections to create harmony. Finding the right group – secular, fun, inclusive – is still the challenge.

~

I came across a 1983 *Télé-Magazine* interview with Dalida that stopped me dead in my tracks. When asked if she would retire (she was fifty), she said no. "I need my job. The anxieties it causes are part of my character: they're necessary." She said her attitude toward work hadn't changed since her student days. "When I finished one assignment, I said to myself, 'And now, what do I do?'"[12]

She could make it through four decades in a fickle music industry, but when it came to retirement, she couldn't do it?

Dalida said stress and anxiety – Type A qualities that can be so beneficial while we're employed – were essential to keeping her going. An article in a 2012 *Human Resource Management Review* described people who don't *have* to make their jobs their lives, but do so anyway, as "bored doing nothing and [working] to keep themselves occupied." Like Dalida, they prefer the stress and anxieties of work over the thought of doing nothing. I identified far too much with this dead pop star. Working or retired, I was always looking for a project.

Dalida typifies the problem of Type A personalities like mine. According to researchers who study Type A retirees, it's not uncommon for us to face challenges with retirement. For many of us, pressure and stress "make life worth living."[10] I don't aspire to be that way, but I am.

In his book, *Retirement: Different by Design*, Dr. Rick Steiner says we A Types have to learn to live differently. Even in retirement, we want to organize ourselves and everyone in our immediate sphere: walking a set route with friends at 6 a.m., yoga class at 9:30, meeting for coffee at 11:15, lunch at 1 o'clock, and it goes on. This rigidity makes us pretty unpopular with partners or with friends who are not A Types. According to Steiner, we have to learn to sleep in (which I struggle to do even now) and take naps during the day. If we join groups, we have to resist running them.

I had not heard of Steiner before Paris and I held pretty rigidly to a daily schedule (which I usually created the night before or early in the morning). I had a hard time letting the city inspire me, allowing myself to get lost (God forbid) or being entirely spontaneous. Bonnie had to take firm control of me so I didn't schedule her days off.

Maybe Dalida could have learned to modify her behaviour, but what happens when a superstar gets too old to perform, when age, failing health and fading looks (remember, this was before Botox) force retirement? Nancy Schlossberg's *Revitalizing Retirement* gave me additional insight into why Dalida couldn't retire and why I felt myself shrinking when I lost the structure or framework in my life: we need to matter. When I crashed, I felt ignored, and my loss of direction and confidence exacerbated that feeling. Alone in Paris with time to think about this retirement life, I understood that part of my need to get back to the arts and to learning was my way of saying, "Dammit, I'm still here. Nope, not dead yet."

Looking at Dalida's life and death put my retirement into perspective. I had choices. I could hole up in our apartment in Paris filled with irrational fears and whine about how things weren't going as planned, or I could just get out there and do something about it. Unlike Dalida, I didn't have an audience. And I had a wonderful partner who loved me and whom I loved. She was funny and interesting and ready for a new adventure.

Dalida coaxed me out of the house. I imagined her spirit following me around, even humming the odd tune in my ear. In chasing her story, I was shaping a meaningful narrative for myself, alone and without an audience. Even now, I often think about her and how her story was a gift when I was scared and lost.

CHAPTER 3

THE APARTMENT ON RUE D'ORCHAMPT: ACCEPTANCE

Dancing, drinking, carousing – they've all been part of Montmartre's past. I shouldn't have been so shocked by our downstairs neighbour's behaviour. Four days into our stay, from 7 in the evening until after 3 in the morning, we lay in bed, eyes wide open, while young men yelled over each other and their thumping music. Sure, we were retired, but Bonnie still had to go to class, and I was waking up regularly with nightmares, often involving getting lost. Crawling out of bed, I felt about the same age as our apartment – 108.

Before being consumed by the city of Paris in 1860 (and inhabited by young men like our neighbour), Montmartre was a quiet little village. In 1875, only thirty years before our building was constructed, a journalist described Montmartre this way: "small, tranquil and silent. One sees narrow, winding streets...houses like one would see in the country...built with buckled and disjointed wood, standing only out of habit." [1]

But as is often the case with areas on the outskirts of a city, rents were cheap and artists, musicians, prostitutes and pimps moved in. By 1876, one of the many defunct windmills no longer milling wheat became an open-air bar, Le Moulin de La Galette, where locals gathered to eat *galettes* (buckwheat *crêpes*) and dance. A regular at the bar, Auguste Renoir staged and painted one of his most famous compositions, *Bal du Moulin de la Galette*, capturing a summer evening's dance on the terrace.[2] Unlike the drunk debauchery below our apartment, the music and dancing in Renoir's portrayal seemed genteel and innocent. I could see that exact windmill from our salon window. I knew the painting well, and as a distraction, exhausted from the parties below, I stared out the window and imagined being part of that scene, posing for Renoir with the men in their boater hats and we women in our best dresses.

My daydream started this way: It's a late afternoon or early summer evening. No longer in my sixties, I'm young, tall and slim, wearing a long, white cotton dress with a ruffle around the starched collar, watching sun dappling the dancers and the men and women chatting around a table.

But imagining myself in that scene led to myriad questions. Bonnie is a portrait artist. She hires models to sit for her and, if she can't get anyone else, I occasionally pose for her myself (under protest). I know how difficult it is to stay perfectly still, even for five minutes. How long did Renoir's models have to hold those poses? I'm particularly consumed with the woman standing behind her seated friend, leaning over to hear the conversation at the table. The stays in that corset must have pushed their rigid ends into her ribs, and her back must have ached at the end of the day. Were the models paid or did they pose for the "privilege" of being in the painter's work? Did they get to eat *galettes*? That might have made it bearable for me, especially if they were stuffed with chocolate.

But there was no chocolate at the end of our sleep-deprived nights, and the bags under my eyes were getting darker and deeper.

Instead of being caught up in the romantic evening breezes of Renoir's painting, we were trapped in the nightmare version of Toulouse-Lautrec's *Le Moulin Rouge* – loud music, cigarettes, gaudy costumes and can-can girls – or at least that's how it felt.

Toulouse-Lautrec captured the frenzy, movement, noise and colour of the famous dance hall in paintings and lithographs featuring dancers Louise Weber (La Goulue) and Jane Avril, always with shadowy male figures in black top hats.[3] If he were alive, I'm sure Toulouse-Lautrec would have painted the same feeling in the comings and goings of the unit below.

I waited a few days to see if our nocturnal neighbour's patterns would change, and when they didn't, I composed an email to the manager of the apartment. My attempts to avoid confrontation, embarrassment or any kind of negative feedback are obvious as I look back.

"I apologize if this email is a little terse," I started, even though I didn't feel the least apologetic. Then I detailed the nights of card playing and loud music.

In the manager's response, he said he didn't know the young man below us, but the owner of our apartment knew his mother. The owner promised the boy's mother would be contacted and the disturbances stopped.

∽

Three months before Bonnie's course started, while the Paris trip was all potential and still abstract, I made finding a place to live one of those projects I was always looking for. I filled hours searching through hundreds of online listings, making charts and organizing spreadsheets. It gave my life direction, even if the search lasted only a few weeks.

When Bonnie and I travel, we like to stay in one location for an extended period and, being budget conscious, rent apartments instead of staying in hotels. But let's face it: what we were looking for in a place we were going to stay in for nine weeks was completely different from what we might live with for a week or two. And renting sight unseen on the Internet poses challenges.

Apartment hunting on the Internet isn't much different from online dating. Photos are out of date, amenities are exaggerated and profiles are filled with phrases meant to seduce, like "romantic studios," "amazing views," "Parisian treasures," and "luxury hideaways." Each apartment, no matter the size or location is pictured in the warm, bright light of a Parisian summer, windows open and curtains blowing gently (cue Edith Piaf singing, "La Vie en Rose").

After days searching websites, I understood a few more things about Paris accommodations. Studios are "romantic" when they are so small, you can never be more than a couple of steps from your partner. "Amazing views" may be small compensation for having to walk up seven flights of stairs. "Parisian" can be code for old and "treasure" for fossilized. One "hideaway" I found purported to be the first studio of a famous Impressionist – but (in teensy letters) it had no heat.

We couldn't afford a place near the Louvre. If prices were any indication, landlords wanted only nobility and lottery winners (and we still hadn't fulfilled that part of our retirement dream). So I looked in Montmartre, near to the instructors' studio. I thought the area's geology might work in our financial favour. Gypsum, the main ingredient in plaster of Paris, was mined for centuries on the *butte* (or hill). Even though they've been monitored by mine inspectors since 1777,[4] the old shafts have left their mark. I read about one street in the neighbourhood that collapsed and caused the wall of a house to fracture. On another street, a geyser suddenly appeared from below and filled the entrance to a house with water. They condemned the building.[5] Could imminent danger result in reasonable rent?

I sent requests to several sites, asking the big questions – the safety of the neighbourhood, the availability of an elevator (barring that, the number of flights of stairs leading to the unit), street noise – but I didn't ask about noisy neighbours.

I finally found an early twentieth-century beauty. In the salon, French chairs covered in plush, peach velvet clustered around a small oval coffee table. Above hung a traditional crystal chandelier. A round pedestal dining table with four high-backed, upholstered chairs completed the room. The kitchen was modern, equipped with a washer/dryer, dishwasher, four burners and a microwave. Finally, the bathroom had the oh-so-necessary tub and, of course, a bidet. After all, this was France.

Even with a discount for staying nine weeks, the apartment exceeded our budget, but we couldn't resist the size and the Parisian light flooding the rooms from four directions. Our rationalizations for spending the money swung from "We're getting old. It may be the last time we can do this" to "We're retired. We deserve it."

The photos were stunning. We posted the site on Facebook. Our friends were impressed. We were so proud. And we all know what pride goeth before.

~

On the plane flying to France from British Columbia, I memorized the most expedient way from Charles de Gaulle airport to our rental in Montmartre: a train from the airport to Gare du Nord, then a taxi to place Émile Goudeau.

We collected our luggage from the carousel and waded through the unlicensed cab drivers waiting like sharks for unsuspecting passengers. I ignored the first two drivers, but when the third offered his services, I was annoyed. "No, we'll take the train, *merci.*"

"The trains aren't running today," he said, smiling. Assuming he was just trying to get a fare, I gave him my best Gallic shrug and pushed an audible expression of dismissive air through my lips. I felt so very French.

Downstairs at the ticket office, the attendant explained major construction on the line had interrupted the trains, but she assured us we could buy a ticket, take a bus to Mitry-Claye – "only ten minutes from here" – where we could catch a different train to Gare du Nord. Did we go back upstairs and take a cab? No. This was a matter of me wanting to have some control. Miss Type A was going to get us to Gare du Nord, dammit.

We took the recommended bus (a twenty-minute ride, standing room only, my luggage pressed painfully into my thighs), waited for the train in the rain, and arrived at Gare du Nord. The taxi dropped us off just below place Émile Goudeau an hour later than expected. For Bonnie, it was an adventure. For me, the legendary Greek Oracle of Delphi might as well have been riding in the back seat with us prophesying doom.

It poured as we bumped our suitcases across the cobbles and up the stone steps to place Émile Goudeau. Even Bonnie's excitement over the famous Bateau-Lavoir, once Picasso's studio, fell on deaf ears. I just wanted to get to the apartment, to a nice warm tub and bed. A hundred metres farther on, our key turned effortlessly in the ox-blood front door of the building. We dragged our cases up the circular staircase one floor to a small landing illumined by a timed light. The second door proved a little trickier. One, two turns before the deadbolt released. Inside a small vestibule and to the right was the final door – the door leading to our perfect Paris apartment. I held my breath, slid the key into the lock and grasped the large, round brass handle. It fell off in my hand.

I gasped. Holding the knob – what else could I do – I pushed open the door and rolled my bag down the hall into the main room. Metal shutters blocked the watery winter light; the dark, fabric wall coverings sucked up any glimmer that might have sneaked through the shutter slats. I turned on the light. It shone from a large, blue, paper Ikea pupa.

The living and dining areas had been switched. In the dining room, a huge Jacobean cabinet topped with a hand-written sign declaring "Do not touch – fragile" loomed over the seating area. Crowded into the diminished space were two additional chairs, and the dining table sported a mismatched leaf. A large sofa bed, covered in florescent, lime-green polyester, bisected the once-grand salon.

The chill of the rain was nothing compared to the chill of disappointment. I knew it had been too good to be true. And we had been so proud. The Canadian voice in my head taunted, "Who did you think you were?"

I opened the shutters in the main room, the hallway and the kitchen. Natural light improves everything, I thought. I moved the couch to increase the space behind the dining chairs, only to find weeks of dust and debris. The ceramic stovetop was bubbled from misuse, and the range hood hadn't been cleaned in who knows how long. None of the doors in the apartment closed, and all the doorknobs were loose. Worst of all, when I turned on the tap for a recuperative bath, all I got was a dribble of water.

I phoned the manager. I kept my voice calm and my manner light as I explained the situation. What I really wanted to do was cry. I somehow felt responsible for the accommodation not being as wonderful as I assumed it would be. I longed for something – anything – to go as planned.

We chatted about how busy his Christmas season had been and how difficult it was to keep good staff. He assured me everything would be set right the next day. I followed up with an emailed note of thanks but attached six photos of the mess we had found just to make sure he took me seriously. I cc'd the email to myself.

That evening, I realized I hadn't opened the bedroom shutter, one of those external, aluminum, rolling blinds. I found the crank and rolled it up.

Suddenly, Paris stretched out below me.

The Eiffel Tower twinkled. Old-fashioned street lamps lit up a park below. Across the park, I looked into glowing windows and over chimney-potted roofs. I whooped with laughter.

"Come and see this," I called to Bonnie. At that moment, I could have been living in a cardboard box and it wouldn't have mattered. This apartment, old and tired, had *the* postcard view of Paris – every old romantic's dream.

As promised, by 3 the next afternoon, our doorknob was re-attached, water gushed into our bathtub, doors closed, and maintenance staff was scheduled to reclean. At 9 that evening, I climbed into bed, balanced my computer on my knees and opened *Les Miserables*. I had missed reading this classic in university, and I never seemed to have the time, when working, to do it justice. Now, in historic Paris with nine weeks stretched out in front of me, I could devote time to the dense political prose. The sheers were blowing gently, just like in the promo photos. Strange. The shutters were closed and the window was latched. I pulled the duvet tighter around my neck.

∾

After my first noise complaint, the next few nights were gloriously quiet. But with the weekend came a party lasting until 4:30 in the morning.

In my more generous moments that evening, I imagined our neighbour channelling the wild spirit of the 1920s jazz clubs in the area: Le Grand Duc or Bricktop's.

The neighbourhood near place Pigalle – where the jazz bars were once the see-and-be-seen places for the artsy set, like Americans, writer F. Scott Fitzgerald and composer Cole Porter, to name just two – makes the Moulin Rouge look like Disneyland. Today, along the boulevard de Clichy, Pussy's advertises table dancing and Lady's, "live theatre" (and I don't think they're performing Molière). The Sexadrome is just steps from Toys Palace, which sits beside Bistrot Cockney. Although clubs have come and gone, I imagine the "feel" hasn't changed much since the '20s and '30s.

One of the first Black, female jazz singers in Montmartre, Ada Smith, known as Bricktop for her red hair and freckles, is no longer a household name. But when she performed in Paris between the First and Second World Wars, she was on a par with the very famous Black American singer and dancer, Josephine Baker.

The English teacher in me loves the story of Bricktop's arrival in Paris. In 1924, at the owner's request, she came to perform at Le Grand Duc. In Harlem, she regularly sang at The Cotton Club, a venue large enough for a full orchestra and musical revues.[6] Le Grand Duc was so tiny that when the performer saw it, she burst into tears and wanted to return to the States. A dishwasher/back-up cook/waiter made her a meal and found her a place to stay. Bricktop's saviour was another American, Langston Hughes, long before he became a famous poet.[7]

Bricktop called the jazz age in Montmartre *"le tumult noir"*[8] and tumultuous described the next party below us. If Bricktop had been performing, I might have enjoyed it.

Slightly odd and twisted, I know, these disturbances gave me something to focus on that wasn't me. The fellow downstairs became my new project. Less reserved and more assertive, my follow-up email to the manager still had a patina of *politesse*. In this way, my personality is an oxymoron – a meeting of two opposites. While I'll panic at small, seemingly inconsequential (to other people) things, like embarrassing myself in front of strangers or not knowing exactly where I am, I have gotten really good at dealing with crises, like cancelled flights and complex paperwork, with a calm cheerfulness that belies the seriousness of the situation. Bonnie thinks it's because I don't want to show weakness in front of others, and maybe she's right.

Neuroscientists have another theory. They believe the manager might be able to thank a small primitive part of my brain called the "amygdala" (a-mig-da-la) for my restraint. Had I been in my thirties, my reaction to our downstairs neighbour's next party might have been much more volatile. But because I'm old (so the theory goes), I was more measured.

The amygdala acts as an alert system, like those warnings we receive on our cell phones in case of disaster. In one study, subjects were shown pictures considered either positive (puppies, kittens) or negative (cockroaches crawling on pizza, people standing over a grave). Researchers scanned the amygdalae of both young and old participants as they looked at these photos. Neither positive scenes nor negative scenes caused the amygdalae in older subjects to react, unlike those of their younger counterparts, who reacted strongly when they saw negative images.[9]

In another study, researchers found when subjects were shown a series of positive and negative pictures, those aged forty-one and up recalled more of the positive images than the negative.[10] But why? At first, they theorized that negative information was harder to process, so we old people didn't bother doing it.[11] But psychologist Susan Turk Charles has shown that, no matter what age, we all react to negative stimuli. Just think of the last time you were complimented by five people on letting your hair go grey, then one person said, "Whoa. That grey makes you look older." What did you remember?[12]

Perhaps, scientists thought, our amygdalae were simply wearing out. But when researchers tested that theory with a series of threats, our amygdalae responded just as powerfully as those of the young subjects.[13]

Psychologist Laura Carsten theorized that as we age, we learn to distinguish between what is potentially harmful and what is merely annoying, reacting to the former and ignoring the latter. This way, we focus more on the positive and keep our emotions on an even keel.[14]

I'm not convinced my amygdala had anything to do with how calmly and politely I complained to our manager. If that part of my brain worked so well when I was in a state of sleep deprivation and noise overload, why didn't it make me feel positive about my retirement and about being in Paris? Why wasn't it saying, "Hey! No big deal. This is just temporary. You've got years to figure out what you want to do."

I guess it's my background in psychology that makes me want to know more about how my brain works. But, of course, brains are complex. I'm sure there are hundreds of theories for why I found myself crashing so far into my retirement. I discovered one answer in a 2010 study of brain structure and personality traits. According to that research, my little amygdala didn't have a chance against all the other parts of my brain not so eager to think positively.

I've known for many years I have traits of a Type A personality. I'm extraverted – assertive, sociable, talkative – all characteristics that could make me sensitive to rewards, both positive and negative. There are three different areas in the brain responsible for this sensitivity.

I'm also a bit neurotic, a trait linked to five systems in the brain (one of which *is* the amygdala.)[15] In brain scans of his subjects, psychologist Colin DeYoung found the volume of parts of the brain associated with neurosis, as well as sensitivity to rewards, was larger in those who identified themselves with Type A traits than in those who didn't.

Moving 3,000 kilometres to a new house in a new city the day after I retired, no wonder my neurotic brain went into overdrive. When my writing didn't work out the way I planned, and when my Plan B didn't go the way I expected, my brain perceived the lack of success as punishment. My amygdala couldn't convince the other parts of my brain they could relax and dial back all those Type A reactions.

And, of course, I couldn't help comparing my stumbling, stop-and-start beginnings to Bonnie's single-minded, successful pursuit of artistic excellence. Did I say I was a *bit* neurotic?

The noisy neighbour downstairs might be a quick fix. Retirement was long term.

~

Ten days into our stay, while finishing breakfast and returning emails, I noticed a small puddle of rusty water on the windowsill – under the same window where Dalida had mysteriously appeared. Too tired to give it much thought, I put it down to the recent snowfall and leaky windows, blotted it up with a paper towel and left the apartment. We had run out of everything edible, and it was time to face the butcher.

Shopping was one of my biggest stressors in Paris. When Bonnie decided to attend the art course, I said I would do the major cooking and housekeeping. Preparing meals, cleaning and laundry were all ways to fill empty hours in the day and avoid any kind of self-reflection.

In my notebook (the same one where I kept all my walking directions), I made a list (in French) of items I needed. I had brought a visual dictionary with me so I could distinguish cuts of meat. I wanted ground beef for a meat sauce. At certain times of the day, the butcher is packed, and the people who work behind the counter selecting, preparing and packaging the cuts are impatient. I looked for ground beef in the cabinet. None. I plucked up my courage. "*Avez-vous de boeuf haché?*" The butcher picked up some stewing beef. "*Haché?*" I asked. And then he said something in rapid French, which I couldn't understand. I didn't know he would grind the stewing beef for me, and he was probably asking me how finely I wanted it minced. Too embarrassed to persist, I said, "*Non, merci*" and left. I went to the butcher around the corner, where I pointed at some chicken legs, held up four fingers to indicate how many I wanted and paid the amount written on the brown paper packaging.

My lack of French added to my isolation. I couldn't understand people on the street or the server in Coquelicot, the shop where every day I'd buy the same baguette because I could read the sign. My brain didn't think quickly enough to ask about ingredients or the price of anything else.

Rue des Abbesses has many small clothing shops, and one day I stopped in and asked (in French) the price of a dress. The saleswoman replied at lightning speed. My face twisted into a mask of confusion and terror. "Would you prefer I speak English?" she asked. She suggested I say, *"Doucement s'il vous plaît"* (literally, "gently please") when people spoke too quickly. A few days later another French speaker said if I used that expression, people might think they should speak more softly. Couldn't native speakers agree on the rules?

In a study on the aging brain, researchers found that when some older people felt their brains were not as good as they once were, they compensated, often by avoiding the situation that made them feel inadequate.[16] It's kind of like avoiding crowds or noisy restaurants when your hearing starts to go.

Now, I'm much better at asking people to speak more slowly, but then, when I was dealing with my own personal doubts, when my self esteem had sunk to an all-time low, I couldn't get the words out and I felt embarrassed. Instead of doing what neuroscientists say we must do to keep our brains active – engage in whatever we are trying to avoid – I often thought to myself, I'll go somewhere I know they speak English.

When I returned home with my chicken legs, the puddle was back. One quick phone call and I greeted our manager, J.N., at the door. He lived up to his dulcet telephone voice. Tall, dark and devastatingly handsome, he swept into the hallway in his full-length, black cashmere topcoat and artfully arranged scarf. He inspected the leak and decided it might be serious since there was a bathroom directly above.

Eight days later, I met the owner of our apartment. The previous day, in my absence, she came in to see the leak and left a note on the dining table. She apologized in advance for the inconvenience. Plumbers would be arriving at 8:30 a.m. to inspect the leak. If I could not be available, she would let them into the unit and stay until the workers finished.

At 8:15 the next morning, the doorbell rang. It was the owner, Mme G. In her eighties, with quick speech and black hair pulled softly back into a roll, her body suggested a life of good meals and fine living. Like many Parisian women her age, she dressed as if she were meeting friends for lunch. A pale peach silky blouse complemented a mid-calf pleated skirt and sensible leather shoes. She walked with a cane. Gracious in a genteel, reserved, Parisian way, she explained in English that she owned our apartment and the one across the little vestibule. They had belonged to her parents. Her niece – Mme G.'s voice soured on the word – owned the leak. I happily left Mme G. in charge.

The note I found on the dining table that evening was even more apologetic. The plumbers located the leak in the main sewer pipe leading from the flat above. They would have to cut open the mirrored column beside our dining table and replace the damaged section of pipe. Would I be available if the plumbers were to come the next day?

I could easily have said no, but still stressed by organizing daily activities and finding my way around the city by myself, I felt a sense of relief. It sounded like a straightforward job, and the plumbers obviously knew what they had to do.

Instead of Mme G., her niece arrived with the plumbers at 9 in the morning. Where Mme G. was soft, niece D. was angular and brittle. I guessed she was in her sixties. She had bright red lips, rouged cheeks, and black hair pulled severely off her face, braided and tucked at the back of her head. In a mash-up of English and French, she said the plumbers had spent eight hours in her tenant's apartment the previous day looking for the leak before pinpointing it. My confidence waned.

She supervised the dismantling of the curtains, rod and mirror, giving directions in clipped tones, then left. I wrote in my journal and sorted some photos while the three workers pulled off the column panel. They titched and sighed. While they knew they would have to saw through the 108-year-old, ten-centimetre metal pipe, they had not brought an extension cord. I thought of my students, who would show up to class without a pen.

Having borrowed a cord from upstairs, they started to cut the pipe. They worked without masks, or protection for their eyes or ears. Even though I wore large noise-cancelling headphones, the screaming saw forced me from the living room into the bedroom.

Eight-and-a-half hours later, the plumbers were fitting the new pipe. They ran in and out with various shaped connectors and additional tools. Bonnie texted saying the transit drivers were on strike, and she'd be late. Mme G. arrived with her second-favourite cakes and a postcard from the grocery store which was featured in the movie, *Amélie*. Her second-favourite cakes? What were we, her second-rate tenants? Was it a comment on the second-rate plumbers or the second-rate apartment? As I pressed my lips to avoid laughing out loud at the absurdity, I tasted the metal dust coating my teeth.

As soon as Mme G. left, I called the manager requesting a deep cleaning be done immediately. He agreed – after only a slight hesitation.

∿

The year before the original sewer pipe was installed in our apartment wall, builders were putting the finishing touches on St-Jean-de-Montmartre, the first church fabricated with reinforced concrete. Authorities were so distrustful of this new technique they stopped construction between 1898 and 1902. The partially built walls stood for two years before authorities gave permission to continue.[17]

I could hear St. Jean's bells from our apartment. They rang every quarter hour, and at 4 in the afternoon I'd often hear the eleven-bell carillon playing "Ode to Joy". On Sundays, the carillon player belted out the entire classic church canon available for eleven notes. I'm almost certain one morning I heard "I Will Survive," but I won't swear to that.

Soundscapes. Paris is filled with them – bundle buggies on cobblestones, tour guides, trash collectors, revving motor scooters. Whereas St. Jean's carillon was music to my ears, the next party below us blared like a klaxon.

At 5:30 in the morning, the blasting music and clamour of party guests were deafening. Because I was a chicken, Bonnie got dressed and went downstairs, ready for a fight. Her amygdala was working overtime. She rang the bell. No one heard it. She banged on the door. When the twenty-something resident answered, he complained – in perfect English – about her banging. (In our bedroom, their voices carried as clearly as the party noises.)

"But you couldn't hear me. I had to bang."

"Well, it's not right," he said.

The frustration elevated Bonnie's tone. "What's not right is being kept up until all hours by noisy neighbours."

"I saw the plumbers and heard the work being done. I thought you had left."

Bonnie's voice increased another fifteen decibels. "You were wrong. We're still here. And we will be here until March. We want to have some peace and quiet while we are."

"I don't give a fuck about you! I don't care. I don't appreciate you raising your voice. I'm an owner; you're just a renter. I'll do what I want."

Bonnie had had enough. "Fuck you. I don't care who you are. We want the noise to stop."

The door slammed. When Bonnie burst into our room, I looked at her and smiled, "That went well." We exploded into laughter, just couldn't help it.

If any phone call had been made to the young man's mother, it hadn't made a difference.

My next email to the manager was bold, containing words like "last straw," "jeopardized health" and "untenable," and finished with a demand for a new place comparable to the one we were in.

He gave us a key to Mme G.'s other unit across the little vestibule to use if needed.

~

Our tickets to the Edward Hopper Exhibition were stamped 5 o'clock Saturday morning. In response to the show's popularity, the organizers arranged to keep the exhibit in the Grand Palais open twenty-four hours a day for the last weekend.

The evening before the show, Bonnie and I ate at the Louvre's food court, then caught the bus back home. Even though it was only 7 p.m., my feet dragged up the staircase. Neither of us had recovered from our lack of sleep. My head ached, and I had started coughing. I pressed the button for the timed light on the little landing outside our door, put the key in the lock and turned it twice. Nothing. I tried again in the opposite direction. Nothing.

I knew D. lived upstairs, but I didn't know in which apartment. Fortunately, her tenant arrived home from work and showed me D.'s door. I knocked.

"Excusez-moi de vous déranger," (Excuse me for interrupting) I said in my best French. I held up my door key. *"Le clé ne marche pas."* (The key doesn't work.)

She looked at me, incredulous. *"Le clé ne marche pas?"*

I stared right back. *"Le clé ne marche pas."*

"Un moment." She retreated into her apartment, leaving me standing at the door, then followed me down one floor. She tried her key. *"Le clé ne marche pas,"* she said. She returned upstairs to get her partner.

Moments later, he joined us carrying the French equivalent of WD40. She said to him, *"Le clé ne marche pas."*

He took her key and tried the lock. *"Le clé ne marche pas."*

I looked at Bonnie and sort of snorted. I could tell, like me, she felt we were in the middle of a French farce. I called our manager, who joined us on the landing five minutes later. He tried his key.

Before he could add to the ludicrousness of the scene unrolling on the landing, I said, "I know. *Le clé ne marche pas.*"

He said half-jokingly he'd never had renters with such bad luck. We all chuckled, but at the same time I thought, I didn't provoke the neighbour downstairs, cause the leak in the pipe or break the lock. I held my tongue.

The manager looked up his usual locksmith's number. In the midst of a dinner party, the locksmith couldn't be there before 10 p.m. I shook my head, no.

"We have to catch a cab at 4:30 tomorrow morning. I've stayed in with plumbers, and have been kept up by noisy neighbours – not that I'm complaining." J.N. called his second choice. He couldn't come until Monday.

"I'm going to call my third choice," he said. "It's not that he's not good, it's just that he's kind of grumpy." Locksmith number three could come.

We waited, five of us crammed onto the two-and-a-half square metre landing, trying to make conversation and repeatedly pressing the timed light.

Choice number three showed up twenty minutes later with an oversized toolkit bungied to the back of his scooter. He and his toolkit squeezed through to the door. He tried our key, sprayed the lock with WD40, tried it again, but with no luck. "I can drill out the lock and return tomorrow to replace it," he said. No longer entertained by the farce, I threw my hands up. "Of course. What choice do we have?" I was a hell of a lot grumpier than locksmith number three.

In those first four weeks, the building on rue d'Orchampt taught me an important lesson. When you're old, you can do what you damn well please. Maybe my aging amygdala was doing a better job than I suspected because the apartment also made me laugh – the only response possible when so many things go wrong.

I didn't see it then, but that apartment was a metaphor for my retirement. While there were many incredible things about it, like its size, location, light and views, there were things that detracted from its beauty, like the leaking pipe and broken lock, and at times made it unbearable, like the noisy neighbour. Everything, however, could be fixed, even if it meant tearing down mirrored panels and drilling out doors. In this early stage of my retirement's resurrection, I needed to do some soul searching – something I'm not good at. I needed to assess the parts of my "house" that were making me miserable. I had to oust the noisy neighbour (the self-critical, neurotic, reward-dependent person who was throwing parties at all hours in my brain); figure out how I could rebuild the hard-working, curious, intelligent, organized person I used to be (who had apparently sprung a leak with time and wear); and rejuvenate the joy that comes from living with light and beauty and space.

CHAPTER 4

SIX HECTARES OF THE LOUVRE: ART AS A PROJECT

In the first weeks of our stay in Paris, the Louvre became my harbour. Afternoons, I could always find Bonnie somewhere in that vast space, watch her draw for a few minutes, then arrange to meet for coffee when she needed a break. On the way home, we'd walk along rue des Abbesses, pick up a baguette at Coquelicot or Le Grenier à Pain and talk about the day.

Partly as an excuse to be in the museum and partly because my restless brain needed to have a project, on my third visit I challenged myself to take on the whole museum – all six hectares of its halls, galleries and staircases.

There was just one snag with the plan. I had never been in an art gallery without my personal guide.

Bonnie and I met when I was twenty-six. I can count on one hand the number of times I had been to the Art Gallery of Ontario before then. My life revolved around skiing, swimming and motorcycling. As an art teacher, Bonnie organized yearly field trips to New York, and she fell in love with the city. From time to time, we flew down for a weekend. She always planned our itineraries, which included a Broadway show and art – lots of art. At first, I could last about an hour in a museum before boredom set in. I understand now my lack of interest was proportional to what I knew. As I learned more, my interest increased, as did my attention span.

By the time we were planning my fortieth birthday – a full week in Manhattan – I had more staying power. Still, I didn't want to spend the whole time in galleries. "I want to make the itinerary this time," I said, thinking that shopping on Canal Street or hanging out in Soho might be fun. Instead, we took our newly purchased rollerblades and bladed up to the Metropolitan Museum of Art (accidentally skating onto the set of *Scent of a Woman* as Robert DeNiro walked across Park Avenue) and then to the Whitney Museum, a collection of twentieth-century art, which was then located on the Upper East Side. Bonnie never lets me forget my itinerary also included the Frick Collection (which features Old Masters), the Museum of Modern Art (MOMA), the Morgan Library (for its illuminated manuscripts) and the Smithsonian Design Museum.

While my love of art grew, I still relied on Bonnie to lead me through exhibits, curating what we saw, explaining movements, pointing out elements and principles of design, and elucidating specific techniques. She knew gossip about artists' lives rivalling *The National Enquirer's* dirt on modern celebrities.

How would I feel about art without her?

Part of rebuilding myself demanded I find out. I needed to put to use the thirty-five years I had spent learning – albeit casually – about art. To push myself even further (because Type A personalities are never satisfied with a *small* challenge), I chose *not* to use an audioguide. I would be left to my own thoughts, my own reactions, no matter how amateurish or uninformed.

I grabbed a map from the information desk, ordered a coffee and a *pain au chocolat* from the café under the glass pyramid, found an empty table and dug my highlighter out of my purse to plot my attack.

The Louvre resembles a giant horseshoe with four levels in the Richelieu wing and three in the Sully and Denon wings. If I had been mathematical, I could have calculated a way to reduce overlap, but I'm not. I decided to work each wing from top to bottom. I took the escalator from the ground floor of Richelieu to the second. I might have admired the view of the Seine through the round windows on the way up, but I can't be sure. I was suddenly overwhelmed by the task I had set myself. Type A people are driven by rewards. What if I walked through every gallery and felt nothing? What if Bonnie was the reason I had come to love art? What if I didn't love art, only Bonnie?

And then I remembered how I felt seeing Gian Lorenzo Bernini's sculpture of Daphne and Apollo in Rome's Borghese Gallery. As Bonnie marvelled at Bernini's ability to portray movement in marble, my thoughts leapt to my mother. She used to read us stories from Grace H. Kupfer's *Legends of Greece and Rome*, a book her mother had given her. The illustrations were photographs of classical sculptures, and Bernini's *Daphne and Apollo* fell out each time she opened the cover. Looking at Apollo stretching forward to capture Daphne as she turned into a laurel tree, I remembered the book's mustiness, the smell of age and damp basements mingled with my mother's breath, and snuggling under my pink-flowered comforter as I felt the horror of Apollo's attack on Daphne.

And then I wondered how it would feel to be twenty-four-year-old Bernini staring at a block of marble thinking of stone becoming flesh becoming bark.

There were so many ways to respond to art. I had to find mine.

I stepped off the escalator and walked into the Medici gallery. Still nagged with doubts about setting such a lofty goal, I couldn't have chosen a worse room. The walls were lined with giant works – each as large as a single-car garage door – commissioned by Marie de Medici to portray her life. Even though the gallery is vast and the skylighted ceiling is double height, the paintings hovered over me; the cast of thousands and the unrelenting Baroque arabesques in Peter Paul Rubens's work pressed in on me.

I want a do-over I thought. I felt like a spoiled kid as I turned around and walked out. I needed to start with a small gallery.

~

Bonnie invented an art game we play when visiting large exhibitions. In each room, we choose one piece we'd like to steal. (We don't say "steal" too loudly; guards get edgy when they hear that word.) Once we've found a piece, we tell each other why it would be worth years in prison.

The conversation might look like this.

Me: "It's a Rembrandt. That makes it worth it right there. But it looks modern. The sitter could be a 1930s New York banker."

Bonnie: "I agree. It's incredible. But come back and look at this other Rembrandt, *The Old Woman Reading*. The light reflecting off the book back up to her face is so complex."

Without some way to focus on the artwork in the Louvre, I knew it would all blur together. So, although it's not as much fun with only one person, after I put my false start behind me, I played this game. Because I lacked my tour guide, I had to pay attention, slow down and reflect. I tried to construct a gallery in my mind, find a spot for each piece I thought "theft-worthy." I imagined that mind-gallery like Gertrude Stein's salon, which I had seen in photographs, crowded with paintings she and her brother collected, but hung as I found them, without paying attention to design or correct height or the relationship to its neighbour. Outwardly, I'm very tidy, but this mental arrangement was more appropriate for the way I felt about my life at that time. Whatever I focused on, I'd imagine telling Bonnie about the content or a specific technique I noticed.

I did worry that I couldn't remember what I had seen. Kathleen Taylor, an expert on adult learning, assures us that when we seniors forget things, they're not lost permanently. "They're just tucked away in the folds of your neurons," she says. While we may not be able to find a word or recall the last book we read, the information is still there somewhere.[1]

But just in case I couldn't "untuck" any details about the paintings I chose, I took photos of my favourite works and their accompanying labels. Later, I would load the photos onto my computer – a folder for each day – and include the information with each piece.

When Bonnie taught art, she showed Sister Wendy Beckett's series, *The Story of Painting*. If you have never heard of Sister Wendy, look her up on YouTube. I fell in love with this buck-toothed, soft-spoken expert in full nun's habit. In a 1997 interview with Bill Moyers, she acknowledged the fears people have about viewing art. She blamed art critics for creating this culture of fear, for instilling in the ordinary gallery-goer a belief that people can't have an opinion about art unless they are highly educated, very bright and know the right language. Stepping into the Medici Gallery on my first exploratory day, I experienced that fear. So in the next gallery, I remembered what Sister Wendy said about how to approach paintings. "Spend time with them, perhaps walk away, come back, look again, let your eye roam around until [the painting] sort of flowers within you, which it will ... and if you've done that and nothing happens, no flowering within, no sudden understanding that this is something magical and mysterious, then that picture isn't meant for you. Try again in a few year's time."[2]

I had already convinced myself that Rubens's Medici paintings would never be for me, no matter how many years passed. But what did "flower within" often surprised me. Exploring a small back room on the top floor of the Richelieu wing that first day, I kept circling back to *Portrait of an Old Woman* by Balthasar Denner, an early eighteenth-century German painter I'd never heard of.

His model's hair is pulled back off her forehead and hidden under a blue silk scarf, the one detail that suggests some wealth. In her, I saw myself – not the twenty-five-year-old I think I am when there's no mirror in the room, but the woman I am now, in my mid-sixties. She looks older than I, perhaps in her seventies, but we share the features of age – disappearing eyebrows, furrowed lines between our brows and over our noses, laugh lines that curl out from the corners of our eyes.

Something riveted me to her. She had my father's eyes, my eyes. As I looked at the masterful execution of the *moiré* in the silk scarf, I realized I had never been to an art gallery with my father. By the time I showed interest in art (I had a boyfriend who drew), my father's Parkinson's symptoms had made it uncomfortable for him to stand still for long periods, and his mind wandered. I tried to predict how my father's retirement might have looked had he been healthy. Tennis, badminton, the piano, travel? He and my mother fought constantly, so whatever he did, I'm sure it would not have included a great deal of "couple time." It would have, no doubt like mine, been tightly scheduled.

I firmly believe I inherited my need for organization from him. Every day at the breakfast table, he asked, "What's on your agenda today?" Before he left for his job as an aeronautical engineer, he'd sit on a chair in the front hall and buff his shoes. Retirement would have challenged his need to organize and schedule as it did mine. Unfortunately, I never had the opportunity to see him face that test.

As I looked at the sitter in Denner's portrait, she looked directly back at me. The artist had given her strength and independence, those qualities I vowed to rediscover in myself. I wasn't there yet, but I had started.

~

My days quickly fell into a pattern. After a half-hour of yoga, I made oatmeal for breakfast. Bonnie made lunches – a baguette with ham, Brie and prune jam – before heading off to school. At first I stuck close to home, learning my way around Montmartre with Dalida's help. The more time I spent alone in the Louvre, the more I wanted to see other artworks, not just the old stuff. I was starting to enjoy my independence, starting to recognize what spoke to me and what didn't (the Medici gallery never did). I planned visits to smaller museums like the Petit Palais or the Musée Jacquemart-André, carefully charting my walks and recording them in my notebook before I left. Then I'd walk to the Louvre or home to do shopping or laundry.

I limited how much I saw in the Louvre, often visiting just one gallery per day. As Sister Wendy said to Bill Moyers, "I think we're all in danger of living part of our lives at zombie level. Art helps one be perpetually 'there.' Art is demanding of your attention."[3] Seeing only a small slice of the collection at one time helped me be "perpetually there."

Two weeks into our stay, Bonnie and I spent a Saturday together in the Louvre seeing some of the northern painters before treating ourselves to lunch in Angelina's, an upscale (over-priced) restaurant in the Richelieu wing. The maître d' seated a twenty-something woman next to us. If the tables in the café had been any closer, she'd have been sitting on my lap. She wore red Mary Janes, the kind we had as girls in the '50s with a swivel strap that converted childish shoes (strap over instep) to grown-up shoes (strap behind heel). Her straps were in grown-up mode.

She had yet to order when she turned to us. "I'm in Paris on a stopover between Singapore and New York." Her delivery laconic, her shoulders slouched and her red-shoed feet stretched under the table, she said, "So far this morning, I've seen the Champs-Élysées, and I've seen the Louvre. I *wasn't* impressed."

Bonnie just about choked on her goat cheese salad, one of the few times I've seen her speechless. I thought of Sister Wendy – living at zombie level, indeed.

We retired folk can luxuriate in extra time, unlike this young woman. I was given a gift of nine weeks to explore this vast collection. Even so, I thought of the galleries I wanted to race through, like the Pavilion Mollien the gallery, where I felt overwhelmed by famous, French, history paintings, including Théodore Géricault's *Raft of Medusa* (which interprets the gruesome end of passengers shipwrecked and left to die on a makeshift raft) and Eugène Delacroix's *Liberty Leading the People* (with Liberty, symbol of the revolution, standing atop the barricades, flag in one hand, rifle in the other). It would have been easy. But I didn't want to go back, to be like the young woman in the red shoes – not impressed.

$\sim$

While I was physically by myself for most of my time in the Louvre, my mind sometimes wanted to host a party of unwanted guests – thoughts about what had gone wrong over the last few years, what I should have done differently, how I used to like myself much better before I retired, how unhappy I would be if I couldn't reboot my retirement – all things I couldn't change or control.

What Sister Wendy was advocating all those years ago was what we're now calling mindfulness – that is, experiencing life as it happens, living in the moment. In a seminar I attended, Sean Pritchard, a Buddhist monk and clinical psychologist, gave a talk on mindfulness-based cognitive therapy (MBCT). He flashed up a slide showing two heads, both looking at a park with green grass and trees. The brain in the first head overflowed with thoughts, most not related to the park. Underneath, the caption read, "Mind full?" The brain in the other head focused on the park's grass and trees. "Mindful," the caption read.

When our minds wander into the past – the should-haves, would haves, could-haves – or into the future – the what-ifs of catastrophic thinking – these thoughts can trigger a stress response, which, in turn, can cause our bodies to react as if there is a physical threat.

Although I hadn't heard about MBCT before I went to Paris, I had studied yoga long enough to know I always felt better when I cleared my head of all my negative thoughts and focused on what was happening in my body and mind in the moment. I started to apply that mindfulness to my gallery visits. Each time I entered a gallery, I fought the urge to rush from one artwork to the next in been-there, done-that mode, just so I could cover my map with yellow highlighter. I took Sister Wendy's advice to heart. I stood in the middle of the room and slowly scanned the walls until I found one piece I liked. Then I had a little conversation with myself. "Why do you like this picture? Is it the subject matter? The colours? The execution?" I tried not to judge the painter – who was I to determine a need for a stronger focal point or a more dynamic composition? Instead, I'd make the most of being in that room at that time, experiencing the art.

I didn't always succeed. Not everything spoke to me. I had the most trouble with religious paintings, but I tried to find something I could appreciate, like the drama in Jean Restout's eight-by-almost-five-metre *Pentecost*. As an onlooker, I'm staring up at the Virgin Mary, high above me on a stage. Around her, the worshippers are awed by her glory, some falling back, others kneeling in prayer. Because of my position below her, I am cast as one of her acolytes, lower than the faithful who surround her. Although I didn't like the painting, I was impressed by the number of women Restout, who painted in 1732, included in his work.

Three years later, during another winter drawing course in Paris, one of Bonnie's fellow students said to me, "I hear you know every artwork in the Louvre."

I laughed. "No." She seemed a little disappointed. "But I visited every open gallery and I know what I liked in each one." I looked at the painting she copied. "I've never noticed the one you're drawing. It's beautiful."

"It's Philippe de Champaigne's *Portrait of Robert Arnauld d'And-illy.*"

I studied the painting for about two minutes. "I love the way his hand appears to be dipping out of the picture frame. It's a hand I'll remember." I added another painting to my personal gallery.

$\sim$

Rooms in the Louvre are easy to miss, especially if they're separated from the main halls. I was into the third week of my challenge when I stepped through a door leading off a hall in the Sully wing. My mind flew back to grade-eleven ancient history class – first desk, third row from the door – and the teacher, Mrs. Bixley, standing behind the slide projector talking about the archaeological dig where she had worked over the summer.

I can still hear the sound of each little square clicking rhythmically into place as she advanced the tray. Pottery fragments flashed on the screen: red male figures on a black background, bowls with sides missing, and an intact plate decorated around the edge. She told stories about each one. Short-haired, wearing no-nonsense shoes with dirt under her fingernails, it was love at first slide.

I liked history in grades nine and ten, but Mrs. Bixley made it come alive with photographs she had taken, rubbings she had done in medieval churches and graveyards. For her, history wasn't just an academic exercise. She sparked a passion for the past I've never lost.

Mrs. Bixley wandered into our backyard as part of a garden tour about seven years before I retired. "When I saw your name in the program, I thought it might be you," she said. But we didn't have time to talk. I regret not telling her the influence she had on me and on my own teaching.

Case upon case, vitrines of Greek, Etruscan and Roman ceramics stretched through six rooms over half the length of the Sully wing. I stood as close to the first case as possible, without leaving nose smudges on the glass, imagining Mrs. Bixley beside me. "That's a *lekythos*," she might have said, pointing to the mostly white vessel, with simple line work in black below the neck, and the faintest picture drawn in ochre on the surface. "Greeks created white ceramics for funerals. This particular pitcher might have contained oil for the deceased's afterlife." I could hear her voice and wondered if she ever stood in this same spot surrounded by the treasures she loved. If I hadn't taken her class, would I have walked through these rooms thinking, "OK, there's another jug, and another one?"

A slightly portly guard smelling of cigarettes walked toward me, then turned and stood about a metre away, hands clasped behind his back. I stopped in front of a cabinet filled with 2,500-year-old vessels of all shapes and sizes. Inky glazes absorbed the light, then cast it back with a mellow glow.

I wanted to run my fingers over the outside of each piece, feel the smooth finish, allow the clay to absorb the heat from my hand.

Did the guard marvel at their craftsmanship? Did he wonder about their past lives? Did he want to know what a young slave girl felt as she filled the water jug at the well? How heavy did it become? Did she carry it on her head? I imagined pouring wine into the *kylix*, smelling the earthiness of fermented grapes, seeing the liquid turn red-brown inside the ebony bowl.

But it was not to be. These vases will never be touched, stroked, used. They are trapped behind glass and alarms and men with little potbellies who smell like cigarettes.

$\sim$

It was impossible to enjoy anything in the Louvre – to pay attention, to be mindful – when my bladder warned me I'd better find a washroom. There are twenty-two women's washrooms in the Louvre. Some are one or two stalls, others much larger. I'm fairly certain in my quest to see the whole museum I visited them all.

I'm going to share a secret – and I will be honest, Bonnie is not happy about this revelation. But it's important to support each other. The Louvre's size is challenging enough to our aging bodies. We shouldn't have to panic about finding facilities.

Tucked away in the northwest corner of the Cour Marly is the best washroom in the museum. The gallery is filled with wonderful garden sculptures from Château de Marly, Louis XIV's leisure residence just outside Versailles. The washroom is in a dead-end corridor off the gallery. It's large – four stalls – so there's rarely a line. A location fairly close to the Richelieu wing entrance makes it especially convenient. Unless I was at the far end of the Denon or Sully wings, I always made my way back there. The only downside is the maintenance staff likes to start their cleaning early. I learned never to leave it to the last minute.

$\sim$

Our noisy downstairs neighbour, leaking plumbing and dysfunctional door took their toll on my health. On week four, I spent two days curled up on the couch. One minute I wanted someone to take care of me, and the next wished everyone and everything would go away. Returning to the Louvre later in the week, I hit a wall. Ironically, it takes energy to focus and remain in the moment and I struggled to do either. I broke my vow to use only stairs and escalators and took the elevator to the French paintings. I confess my mind started to buzz with plans for our daughter's upcoming visit, and I walked through at least eight rooms before I saw anything.

I muttered something to myself like, "Come on, Sue. You're here. Remember Sister Wendy. Focus."

The first painting I noticed was Hubert Robert's 1796 *Refurbishment Project of the Grand Gallery of the Louvre,* in which he imagines a post-French Revolution Grand Gallery with natural light flooding through skylights, pictures hanging in tiers along the walls, and console tables displaying vases and other artifacts. Busts sit on plinths, and full-sized sculptures are raised on daises in the middle of the room.

The painting shows three artists. The first (apparently Robert, himself), sitting in front of Raphael's *The Holy Family,* copies the masterpiece. A second artist, dressed in hose, boots and a red cape, sits on the floor. He leans against one of the plinths for support and props his sketchpad against his crossed leg.

A third artist perches on a straight-backed chair, knees against a footstool. Dressed in a dun brown, floor-length dress, a shawl covering her shoulders, and a hat with ribbons tied under her chin, she leans over her drawing board, which she is supporting with her left hand. Each of the artists is busy, but relaxed and unharried by crowds.

I felt a little jolt of pride thinking of Bonnie, the modern day embodiment of something Robert envisioned 200 years ago.

Fortunately, Bonnie doesn't have to wear a full-length dress and bonnet; unfortunately, she is not allowed a large drawing board. She is limited to a 40 × 56 × 5 cm. portfolio in which she must carry her drawing board, paper, pencils and a small collapsible stool. Unlike the large, hard-backed chairs featured in Robert's painting – which Bonnie could only dream about – her stool is the most fundamental available. It has crossed metal legs between which, when opened, stretches a small piece of canvas, about 20 × 30 cm.

Bonnie was sixty-seven when she accepted the position in the Paris course. While to me, her retirement exemplified "practically perfect," I needed to remind myself that even the most fulfilling retirements have ups and downs. She had applied the previous year but failed to get in. Her blue funk lasted for a couple of weeks, then she hired a model and practiced, applying the following year with a much stronger submission. She does worry she won't be able to improve, and this fear increases as she moves further into retirement.

There are times when fear overwhelms even her Pollyanna personality, flinging her into a despondency that's difficult to surmount.

But if we can believe the neuroscientists, she should be able to keep improving as long as she works at her art, thanks to the brain's ability to create neural paths, rewiring itself in response to new experiences and learning. According to adult-education expert Dr. Kathleen Taylor, as long as adult learners disturb their established brain connections – "jiggle their synapses" – by confronting established opinions and ways of doing things, the brain stays in tune.[5]

If the scientists are right, every time Bonnie applies the information she's learning in classes to her drawing, she's shaking up her neurons.

The physical challenges of pursuing her art proved more difficult than the intellectual. Four days a week, she hefted her portfolio (about three kilograms fully loaded) down the 188 steps into the Abbesses métro station and onto the train. Taking the subway with riders crammed together like pages in a book tested her agility. Unless she could maneuver herself to a position at the end or side of the car and slip her portfolio behind her, she became a one-woman obstacle course.

Once in the Louvre, the challenges continued. She'd lift her portfolio and purse onto the x-ray machine's belt and retrieve them (thankful the guards had not discovered the blade she had hidden so she could sharpen her pencils) before schlepping her equipment to her gallery. With her pencils laid out beside her, she'd settle onto the stool's fabric, which had been stretched so much the metal bars dug into her hips. Propping the drawing board somewhere between the top of her thighs and her groin, she'd steady it with her left hand as she drew. Every time she had to use the toilet, she packed away all her gear, including her stool. Nothing could be left even for a few minutes.

I've walked around the museum with Bonnie as she's searched for things to draw. Sculptures have to be large enough for her to maintain a comfortable distance and still see details with her bifocals. If the red-caped man in Robert's painting were going to draw one of the marble busts from his position on the floor, he wouldn't see much of anything. And if he moved closer, he'd be craning his neck at an impossible angle.

All three of the artists in Robert's painting are younger than Bonnie. They aren't wearing glasses, and their joints probably didn't creak or get stuck in one place when they sat for too long.

Robert imagined one thing accurately. Behind each artist in his painting, there is an observer. These days, the onlookers not only watch the artists, they take pictures – usually without asking. What Robert didn't envision were the crowds in the Grand Gallery. On a normal day, there are hundreds of people in that gallery. It is, after all, one of the most popular in the museum, the most direct route to the *Mona Lisa*. Artists who draw in crowded places like the Grand Gallery have to be patient with people standing over them, or between them and what they're drawing, blocking their view.

Even quiet rooms are rarely empty. One afternoon, a large tourist group entered the Hall of the Caryatids, where Bonnie was copying a sculpture of a satyr playing a flute. As she drew, the group of about fifteen people gathered around her stool. The leader leaned in from the side and started pointing at different areas of the drawing, talking about Bonnie's technique. Her finger hovered a centimetre from the soft, easily smudged graphite. Terrified, Bonnie froze until the art lesson ended. There followed no apology for the interruption, no "thank you very much," just a few moments of further staring and nodding, and on they moved, following their guide.

In that same gallery, one of the guards took it upon herself to critique Bonnie's work. First she suggested there were more interesting statues in the gallery than the one Bonnie had chosen. Then she questioned the placement of Bonnie's stool. "I think the light is better, just over here." Finally, as the drawing progressed, the guard made some suggestions on how it could be improved. Luckily, Bonnie is even tempered and not easily offended. I wonder how Hubert Robert would have reacted had the woman behind him leaned over, pointed and said, "I'm not sure you've got that background quite right."

~

When our daughter D'arcy came to visit, we were five weeks into our stay. By that time I had been to the Louvre twelve times, eleven of those by myself. It's hard to say how many galleries I had seen, since one subject – like French paintings – might span forty galleries. I spent longer in some rooms than others, and I returned several times to a few displays, like the case of Egyptian musical instruments. I loved the curves of the stringed instruments, but just as mesmerizing were the crisp and sculptural shadows they cast in the case.

The initial idea of seeing the whole Louvre grew from a need to fill time and be physically near Bonnie. Now, I went to the gallery even when she was in the studio.

But I still missed being with others during the day. A teacher is never alone, from the time she steps into the workroom in the morning until she drives out of the parking lot in the afternoon, and the extrovert part of my brain loved company. In addition to morning classes in the studio and afternoons in the Louvre, Bonnie spent evenings rereading her notes and working on her drawings, trying to apply theory to practice. Sometimes I offered transcription services and typed as she dictated in an alien language (using terms like "skiagraphia, and non-parallel irregular planarity"). I interrupted every few seconds. "How do you spell *that*?" She put herself under tremendous pressure to perform, even working through weekends.

Luckily for all of us, Bonnie had a week off school during D'arcy's visit. I am still a little unnerved at how quickly I slid into old patterns: slowing down and mindfulness be damned; I had a tour to organize. Skyping with D'arcy, I said, "Make a list of ten things you want to do when you're here." When she sent it, I mapped out the week.

On her fourth day, I organized a cemetery tour, a visit to St. Sulpice (made famous by Dan Brown in *The Da Vinci Code*) so she could walk the Rose Line, followed by a stroll along the Left Bank and over one of the most famous bridges in Paris – the Pont Alexandre III – to the Petit Palais. D'arcy loves Art Nouveau and I had found several brilliant examples in that museum.

We started out at 9 in the morning but took so long at our first stop that we had to grab a quick lunch at an overpriced café on the Left Bank before going to the church. The bridge was another two-and-a-half kilometres away. While I had planned the Louvre trip for later in the week – it ranked number ten on D'arcy's list – at 5 o'clock, Bonnie had the bright idea to walk over to the museum, grab a snack and get D'arcy free admission after 6, a privilege that comes with membership. It would have been so easy for D'arcy to say, "I'm exhausted. Let's go home." I felt a little like that myself.

When we entered through the members only line, I felt at home. No longer the follower, I led the way. Because Bonnie sat in one gallery to draw, she didn't know her way around. I, on the other hand, could give directions to lost tourists. *Napoleonic Rooms? Up the stairs from here and turn to your left. The Egyptian mummies? Straight down this hall and turn left at the end. You'll go down a set of stairs, then back up.* Every time I helped someone out, I felt a little of my old confidence coming back.

I thought we should limit our initial tour to three pieces: the *Venus de Milo*, the *Mona Lisa* and Gericault's painting of the *Raft of the Medusa*. But, of course, as we walked through the Etruscan gallery, Bonnie said, "Just stop for one second and look at this." Bonnie is always in charge in museums so when, three cases later, I called D'arcy over and said, "You've got to see this little statue. It's amazing," I even surprised myself. We zig-zagged through that gallery, Bonnie pulling her one way, me another and D'arcy snapping pictures.

Up the stairs, just past the rotunda leading from the Denon to the Sully wing, Bonnie showed D'arcy a wall mounted with carved limestone pieces, once part of a building's decorative frieze.

"These are from the Parthenon."

D'arcy started to cry. "Not only did I never think I would come to Paris," she said between sniffs, "I never thought I would see something from the Parthenon, from ancient Greece." And she welled up again.

I had walked by these sculptures at least six times without stopping. If it hadn't been for D'arcy, I may never have taken a second look. Emotionally, even artistically, the sculptures hadn't done anything for me. D'arcy's reaction jolted me. A parent never wants to see her child cry, but D'arcy's were tears of joy and wonder. Even in the short time I had been there, I had started taking the Louvre for granted. Maybe Sister Wendy was talking about this type of attitude when she spoke of living at zombie level. Seeing these carvings through D'arcy's eyes reminded me how profoundly privileged I was to be in this city and to see its treasures.

A few moments later, we were alone with the *Venus de Milo*. "Wednesday night. I told you it would be empty." Bonnie puffed out her chest. I rolled my eyes and shook my head. D'arcy just smiled.

Continuing down the length of the gallery, Bonnie wanted to show D'arcy something that had made *her* cry. The stone is about twenty centimetres high and ten wide. It could have been part of a funeral marker, according to the museum's note.

The painting is very faint. A woman lies on a divan. Her eyebrows and eyes are highlighted with kohl, Egyptian-style, and her hair is piled on her head. Her left arm lies alongside her; her hand rests on a table that holds a vase. Standing to her left is a little boy, presumably her son, wearing a shirt that comes just to the top of his legs, and socks (or boots) halfway up his calves.

Although rare for us to be in a gallery together, I had been with Bonnie the day she saw this little painting, the same day we met the young woman with the red shoes.

"Look at this," she called to me. "It's fully rendered. And the people," she could hardly contain herself. "They're not stylized. They're three-dimensional. The artist is creating value, depth and form."

"So?" I said.

"So?" Bonnie looked at me, eyebrows raised. Her next six sentences were delivered so quickly even I didn't take a breath. "People thought Greeks didn't know how to draw realistically. It's just not true. In Byzantine times, Christians dictated that artists couldn't represent humans except in stylized fashion. Of course, we've seen Roman figurative paintings from Pompeii and Egypt, but I can't recall ever seeing anything remotely like this. Even today, some religions don't allow the depiction of natural life, including the human form."

My reaction to this painted stone reinforced what I discovered on our first big trip after retirement. Reading the label, I assumed the mother and child died at the same time and someone commissioned this tribute for the two of them. I imagined games the child played, the contents of the jar, what the mother thought about her son and how they died. The little painting moved me, but never once did I think, "How wonderfully realistic these figures look." It made me think about how I had been connecting to the paintings and sculptures I had seen in the four weeks leading up to that night. Clearly, it was story.

Had anything made me cry? No. I began to think I lacked the art-crying hormone. Then I had this thought:. I had seen most of the Louvre by myself. But spending time with D'arcy and Bonnie, getting excited about showing them something I admired, listening to them gush about different works, made my experience deeper. Like we burrowed into some unexplored part of ourselves and intensified each others' experiences by doing so.

Every retirement how-to I read talked about the necessity for partnerships to evolve, and this time in Paris pushed Bonnie's and mine in a new direction. In my first few weeks in Paris, I equated independence with being alone and feeling lonely. But gradually, I began to enjoy my own company and revel in my discoveries. After a day in the Louvre, I'd show Bonnie the photos of my favourite works. Since she rarely left the gallery where she drew, she experienced the Louvre vicariously, curated by me. The role reversal was empowering.

This evening impressed upon me the balance I needed to achieve between independence in our relationship and interdependence – that sense of connectedness that makes us feel safe enough to pursue our dreams.

Gaining independence was essential to make the next stage of my retirement work, but I realized that in thirty-five years of seeing art with Bonnie we had created a bubble of intimate time in a public place. We shared a virtual gallery of thousands of works from hundreds of museums. Looking at a painting or sculpture together was like an emotional and intellectual embrace. That embrace enfolded me through my time alone in the Louvre, not confining me, but protecting me as I stepped out on my own.

~

Two weeks before returning to Canada, I meandered through the galleries of Egyptian antiquities toward the Hall of the Caryatids before meeting Bonnie for coffee. The rooms on the ground floor of the Sully wing remind me of the Royal Ontario Museum I knew as a child, long before interactive, overly curated exhibits. Room six is one of ten small, linked rooms filled with cases of Egyptian objects. In a case devoted to writing implements, an ivory scribe's palette – about 30 cm. long by 2.5 cm. wide and as thick as my baby finger – stopped me in my tracks. It looked like a wooden pencil case I treasured as a child, where the lid slid back to reveal the pencils. With use, the inscription on the ancient ivory case had almost disappeared, but the two inkwells at the top of the palette remained. One had contained red ink – I could see traces of colour. The second still held a cake of black ink, which, according to the Louvre's website, could still be used.

Into a slot down the centre of the case were slipped four reed pens. The case, these pens and the ink were between 3,000 and 3,500 years old. Each reed was so thin. How did the scribes hold them? It would have been like writing with a toothpick. I wanted to pull one of the reeds from the case, spit on the end, scratch it across the cake of black ink and write my name just to find out.

I'm not sure if at that moment I decided to make a serious attempt to start writing again, but I know it planted a seed. Stories live everywhere in the Louvre: in the artwork, in how each piece came about, in who created it and who had owned it. My own history bumped up against every gallery I entered, each piece of art I studied, every sculpture I walked around, every object I focused on.

I kept circling the cases dedicated to writing, thinking about the joy Bonnie got from painting and drawing, and the joy I experienced before retiring when I authored educational books. The early morning free-writing helped me observe myself in relation to the world and think aloud about that relationship. But those positive feelings stood in stark contrast to the fear I developed when I tried to freelance. While I loved the act of creation, the pressure of finding stories and, even worse, pitching those stories overwhelmed me.

In *Happy Retirement: The Psychology of Reinvention*, Kenneth Schultz, a specialist in issues related to aging and the workplace, recommends pursuing one of the arts in retirement because of the neurological benefits for our brains. He suggests, however, choosing one that has intrinsic rewards. He cites writing as an example, saying if our aim is to create a bestseller, the probability of frustration and feelings of failure increase.[6] Writing for its own sake – whether or not it develops into a great, new career – is the healthiest option.

His advice made me reflect on my original post-retirement goal – to have a freelance career. I realize now I hadn't chosen it based solely on the pleasure I got from writing, but because of the external recognition I assumed would come from it. Thinking back to psychologist Colin G. DeYoung's work with Type A personalities, the need-for-reward parts of my brain were probably working overtime.

As I looked at the scribe's pens, I knew I wanted to get back to writing without being so obsessed by the outcome, but rather enjoying the simple reward that comes from putting pen to paper.

~

The Greek ceramics gallery drew me back on several occasions. I'd like to think the poet John Keats stood in front of a vitrine admiring similar vessels, inspiring "Ode on a Grecian Urn." When I first read the poem, I wasn't much older than the poet when he wrote it. His description of lovers frozen in hot pursuit, never able to touch one another, titillated me. There is such sexual tension in the lines, "Bold Lover, never, never canst thou kiss/Though winning near the goal."

How things change. Reflecting on these lines now, older and maybe more cynical, I know anticipation is often more exciting than reality. These young lovers will never be disappointed in love or in life.

Keats never reached retirement age – dead from tuberculosis at twenty-five – and understood all too well that each generation has a short time on earth. I'm moved by his observation: "When old age shall this generation waste/Thou shalt remain, in midst of other woe/Than ours." I am the generation that is wasting and these vases and urns will still exist long after I'm gone. But unlike the men and women who, in the early nineteenth century, lived on average to age forty, my life expectancy is over eighty. I am not going to be around forever, but I could live for another twenty years and I don't want to spend those years wondering "what if?"

The six hectares of the Louvre taught me something about aging. I don't want to be put behind glass, be a figure frozen on a Grecian urn. I want to pursue new dreams while I can.

The folds in my Louvre map are reinforced with tape. Rooms are highlighted in different colours – yellow, pink and green – and scribbled notes remind me of a special exhibit or a painting I had to revisit. I keep it as a reminder to quiet my brain, pay attention and be mindful. Its fragility reminds me how vulnerable I felt starting my six-hectare quest, riding up the escalator to the third floor of Richelieu. But when I look at all those halls, galleries, staircases, I understand the role they played in pushing me toward independence and helping me redefine what my relationship with Bonnie was, and is, becoming.

CHAPTER 5

LESSONS IN STONE: RECLAIMING MYSELF

Sometimes something comes out of the blue that we didn't know we needed, something that nudges us back towards ourselves. In my case it was Parisian graveyards.

In retirement, time is fluid and schedules less rigid, a challenge for my need for structure. Believing in our ability to control our environment is essential for our general well-being.[1] Before retirement, I probably overestimated the amount of control I had in my job and in my abilities to succeed. But when I quit work, others seemed to be in control – in the case of freelancing, editors, and in the case of the choir, everyone except me.

At the beginning of our trip, our dream apartment in Paris was falling apart, I found grocery shopping stressful and, apparently, I didn't know the first thing about French manners. So, when I found an opportunity to exercise control, I jumped at it. The list that D'arcy sent me before she arrived, the one that included the church of St. Sulpice (number three) and the Louvre (number ten), ranked Jim Morrison – lead singer for The Doors – number one. To see him, we would have to go to Père Lachaise cemetery.

As children, we're always trying to impress our parents. As a parent, I wanted to impress D'arcy. Determined not to waste any precious time on our visit to the cemetery, I planned a reconnaissance mission. That's how I found myself opening our front door to the snowiest day Paris had seen in decades. Most Parisians, familiar with inevitable bus cancellations and snarled traffic, stayed home.

Not me. I had a plan, dammit, and besides, I'm Canadian. There's never bad weather, just bad clothes. A little snow wasn't going to deter me.

Père Lachaise lies in the 20th *arrondissement*, the most easterly part of Paris. Getting there meant taking two trains, neither of which I was familiar with. Unlike so many people who revel in losing their way, I am not happy when I don't know where I am. I lived in the Toronto area for fifty-five years. About a year before we moved out west, I came up from the subway in the east end of the city, and didn't know which side of the street I was on (north or south) or which way to turn to get to a friend's house. With great embarrassment (and I admit a few tears) I called Bonnie at home, and she "walked" me to my destination.

To ensure an uneventful trip to Père Lachaise, I had consulted Google for the closest métro station and my *MapGuide* for directions to the cemetery, and I'd carefully written all that information into my notebook. Still, the needle on my virtual anxiety meter hovered between high and extreme.

Stepping onto our street, I was struck by silence. Ten centimetres of snow had transformed the city into a fairy land. The little concrete bollards lining the curbs sported puffy elf hats, and the cobblestones wore a soft, white carpet.

But in beauty lay treachery.

"Shit." My curse echoed down the alley. With so many inconsiderate dog-walkers on Paris streets, I was constantly vigilant. But the snow disguised this little pile. I pawed at the curb, scraping the brown mess from my boot.

I hugged the buildings skirting place Émile Goudeau, then clutched a narrow metal railing before descending five steps to the street on the other side of the park. Rue Ravignan could give the streets of San Francisco or the climb to Everest's base camps a run for their money. As I picked my way down the slick sidewalk, more than once I wished I had brought those crampon-like contraptions for the soles of my boots. It took me twenty minutes to walk three blocks to the subway.

I waited on the platform, the lone rider.

Even though I had been using a paper map and walking most everywhere, I must not have spent enough time developing my GPS neurons – those cells that create cognitive maps in our brains and help us get our bearings. Either that, or my neurons were simply slow learners. At the top of the stairs leading from the métro station nearest the cemetery, I couldn't tell which way the subway exit faced and which way I had to walk. I had to rely on a street sign (it was the size of the tiny sign indicating the entrance to Montmartre cemetery) for the correct direction. Luckily this time I saw it.

The warmth leaking from the shops along the boulevard had melted the snow in a narrow strip directly in front of their windows. As I walked, I placed one foot in front of the other, sticking to this safety zone. Although only one block from the subway, it seemed forever before I saw the cemetery wall and found the grand entrance. I pushed on the huge, green iron gates. They didn't give. I had a flashback to the first day I had tried to find Dalida's grave in the Montmartre cemetery. But I had no doubt this was the main entrance to Père Lachaise, with its semi-circular walls set back off the street. Had I misread the opening times? My anxiety needle edged up a few notches, I had a massive hot flash and then a lump rose in my throat. I returned to the boulevard. If I just kept walking, surely I'd find an open gate. I *had* to.

The sidewalk had its own set of ecosystems. Sometimes it was clear, then slushy, then my heel skidded out from under me as I hit black ice. As much as I enjoyed the air and the way the snow transformed the streetscape, the muscles in my legs and back were on constant alert and there was no sign of an opening in the three-metre stone wall. When I hit the end of the graveyard, I turned right and continued a kilometre along a street that stretched across the cemetery's width. Without any sun, the footpath was still covered in snow. Unlike the dry cold of British Columbia's Interior, that morning was damp and bone chilling. The wall to my right ran higher and higher along a rocky cliff, the whole endeavour further and further from my grasp.

This had not been in the plan. I was in uncharted territory. I turned at the first street I came to, keeping the wall on my right.

The other side of the narrow road was lined with older apartment buildings, their windows protected by wrought-iron bars and their metal shutters pulled tight. It was grey and deserted. After what seemed like thirty minutes, but was probably only five, I found another major entrance – Père Lachaise's back door. The gates were ajar and a *gardienne* stood in front of the opening in a sort of "at ease" position.

A hearse pulled up to the gates. The driver approached the guard and, while I couldn't hear what was being said, there were raised voices and wild gesticulations. As the driver returned to the vehicle, I tentatively said (in my best French, remembering what the last *gardienne* had taught me) "*Bonjour.* Is the cemetery open?"

"No," she responded in English. "The snow."

The hearse backed out of the driveway. My heart dropped to my stomach. My brain jumped into catastrophic mode. *I've come all this way. I risked my neck to get here. I have to get into that cemetery. I can't wreck D'arcy's holiday. I need to find Morrison's grave.* I was like a crack addict willing to do anything for her next fix.

I found myself considering ways to distract the guard and sneak through the opening. *Maybe if I wait for another hearse and while she talks to the driver…*Then, watching the hearse drive away down the street, the absurdity of the situation slapped me in the face. *I can come back. Jim Morrison isn't going anywhere.*

I retraced my steps to the major avenue, wondering if maybe controlling how I felt on the inside was more important than trying to control the outside. Mine were still the only footprints on the shady sidewalk. Across the street, most of the metal shutters on the storefronts were locked and the handlebars and seats of scooters parked on the street were piled with snow. I imagined parents letting their children sleep in and going back to bed themselves with the luxury of an extra hour or two to make love.

My locus of control did not extend to cemeteries or the weather, and I laughed out loud. Snow in Paris could stop even the dead.

$\sim$

I needed to modify how I reacted to the unexpected, but I wondered if I could change how I was wired. Panic and catastrophic thinking have been my go-to reactions for as long as I can remember. I had an excellent role model – my mother. She had many wonderful qualities, kindness and a big heart being just two of them, but she did not handle stress well. One night, when my brother missed his curfew, she actually phoned all the local hospitals checking for accident victims.

Neurologists believe we strengthen neural pathways when we repeat a response to an event, meaning the more often we panic in a stressful situation, the more likely we are to repeat that behaviour the next time we're stressed.[2] I think my mother's neural pathway – the one that ran between something-is-not-quite-right and full panic mode – was a superhighway. I recognized that pattern in myself and knew it wasn't healthy. I needed to make a change. Luckily, neurologists also say we can create new paths. Just like Bonnie jiggling her synapses in the Louvre, we form new connections between our neurons when we learn something or even change the way we normally do things. And this ability doesn't seem to be hampered by age. So with some work, I should be able to change my response to the unforeseen and alter the way I view past events.

Of course, I could come back to Père Lachaise. I could find Jim Morrison even if it meant delaying my regular visits to the Louvre. If the dead had to be flexible, surely I could be too.

With a practice run under my belt, my second attempt a few days later went flawlessly. I climbed the stairs from the subway with confidence. The sidewalks were clear and dry and I strode past several shops I hadn't noticed on the first attempt – a paint and wallpaper shop, an undertaker (*pompes funèbres* sounds so much nicer), a bistro – and through the big, green gates of the main entrance.

Inside, where cemeteries post a blow-up of their paper guides, I stood pen in hand and wrote down the names of the cemetery streets I had to follow. If I got lost, I thought, at worst, I could follow the smell of pot. Surely some of his acolytes would be there already.

While the snow had disappeared from the cobblestones in the middle of the highly cambered streets, the edges defined treachery.

I hit Division 6 of the cemetery from the rear and stepped through to Morrison's site. But – and I'm going to sound really old here – what a mess! A barrier, the kind set up to keep pedestrians off the street during a parade, surrounded the front of the grave. Down the sides, orange construction tape draped slackly between pylons. Graffiti – personal tags, signatures and dates, drawings of marijuana leaves – covered the entire side of the neighbouring tomb. Morrison's headstone, dwarfed by the grand monuments surrounding it, was just large enough for his name and dates. And the entire grave had sunk beneath ground level. I don't know what I expected, but it wasn't that.

A few years earlier, Bonnie and I searched for traces of my ancestors in Northern Ireland. In 1837, my great-great-grandfather Joseph Patton came to Canada from a farm near Clogher. Unlike so many Irish immigrants, he left before the potato famine. Joseph served briefly with the loyalist militia in 1837 against the rebellion led by William Lyon Mackenzie (grandfather to William Lyon Mackenzie King, Prime Minister of Canada during World War II). For his service, my great-great-grandfather received 100 acres in the Hills of Mulmur, north of Toronto. No one knows whether or not that promise of land lured him to Canada.

I think about the uncertainty I felt when my retirement dreams melted away and imagine the doubts that must have crept over Joseph and his young wife, holding their infant son as Ireland disappeared from sight. Or did they embrace the unknown, relish possibility? Did I come from a line of risk-takers, people who just got on with reinventing themselves?

Here's the thing about reinvention: it's easier when you're young. When you're old, missteps feel more calamitous. You can't be sure how many more chances you'll get.

In Clogher, Bonnie and I searched the rows of granite monuments for Pattons, then combed the area with longer grass and smaller headstones. The farther away from the church, the smaller the stones until only small, flat plaques lay hidden in the long grass, none of them with the Patton name. Joseph Patton escaped poverty by starting a new life in Canada – in fact, his grave is marked by a beautiful headstone in a cemetery near Alliston, Ontario. Those who stayed behind weren't so fortunate.

I turned to Bonnie. "Do you remember what Mary Walsh said on that episode of *Who Do you Think You Are* when she travelled to Ireland looking for her roots?"

Bonnie nodded. "The poor tread lightly on the earth."

$\sim$

If Jim Morrison hadn't been rich and famous, he and his dilapidated grave would have been removed. In Paris, a grave is leased for a renewable period of five to fifty years or "in perpetuity," and payment is per square metre depending on the length of the stay. When the lease expires, the remains are removed, buried in an ossuary on the property, and the grave is re-used.

Graves leased in perpetuity depend on descendants for their upkeep. I always felt a little sad when I saw a yellow ochre sign on a grave saying "*Cette concession fait l'objet d'une reprise administrative. Prier de s'adresser au bureau de la conservation.*" The sign means that unless someone comes forward, claims the site and refurbishes it, the remains will be removed and the unattended grave will be re-assigned. Eternity has an entirely different meaning in Paris.

In 2001, panic broke out amongst Morrison's followers, who thought the thirty-year lease on his grave would expire. French officials assured the public his grave was *une concession perpétuelle* – there forever. Even though his grave is sinking and graffitied, *indécent* and *délabré* (grounds for removal for all other graves), they aren't going to eject one of their biggest attractions.[3]

A week later, in the morning before we took D'arcy to the Louvre, I proudly marched her straight to Morrison's grave, and also gave precise directions to several lost Morrison pilgrims. That week proved a turning point for me. Our apartment woes had ceased, my health had improved, my mindfulness project in the Louvre was going well, and travelling alone around Paris – to the Musée d'Orsay, the Pinacoteque gallery, and the three large shopping havens, (BHV, Printemps and Galeries Lafayette) – had boosted my confidence.

"I wish I could get closer," D'arcy said as she leaned against the barrier. "Damn. And I wish I had some Jack Daniels to pour over the headstone." Apparently, this is another ritual followed by fans.

Bonnie and I stood a few steps away. We were lucky to have her with us. At sixteen, D'arcy took a bottle of acetaminophen, then changed her mind and told us what she had done. We rushed her to the hospital, where they pumped her stomach. A year later, she moved out of the house. She was twenty-two and pregnant when we re-established contact.

Watching D'arcy revelling in her moment with Morrison, I thought of the profound shift in our relationship from the young adult who fought against rules and responsibilities (and partly, I'm sure, because her mothers were gay) to the mature woman who loved to travel with us, looked after our home when we were away and took such pride in her own daughter and granddaughter.

I also admired her ability to deal with the unexpected. When her daughter was less than a year old, D'arcy left her abusive partner and became a single parent. After moving from Ontario to Alberta, she met and married the man of her dreams. Then, eight years later, he suffered a physical and mental illness that changed him into a person she no longer recognized. Although she resisted leaving, she finally moved to British Columbia and started again. Like my Irish ancestors, she uprooted herself without any idea of what the future held and carried on. Now, she's settled in her own home with a responsible job and a paid-off mortgage. She's an inspiration.

Shakespeare said, "Security is mortal's chiefest enemy." I started teaching when I was twenty-four and retired thirty-one years later. Other than leaving my husband, moving into my own apartment, then moving in with Bonnie and the girls, my life has been fairly straight (no pun intended) forward. Despite changing jobs seven times, I never left my chosen career.

Unlike D'arcy's move to BC, ours was carefully orchestrated and (according to retirement books and articles) we did it for all the right reasons: downsizing to a more affordable house; shortening the flights to New Zealand; being closer to the mountains for skiing. We chose a city with a university and an arts presence, and a downtown apartment from which we could walk to everything. Granted, we left friends and family behind, but knew we could find a new community and meet up with family by Skype or as we travelled.

I took the security of my pre-retirement life for granted, so when post-retirement didn't go exactly as planned, I floundered. By rethinking the results and significance of past events, we can alter our brain's responses to similar events in the future, according to psychologists.[4]

You'd think studying psychology for four years would have made this simple strategy a no-brainer. In the first years of retirement, I had ventured further afield and reacted less urgently to unexpected detours. But later, I was reticent to take risks or try anything new. Yes, my self-esteem took a battering, and I felt defeated by apparent rejection. But I hadn't been physically injured when magazines rejected my work or when the choir folded. All my basic needs were still looked after. I still had friends and family who loved me. Including D'arcy. I studied her. Wrapped in her black, belted coat with the faux fur collar, her long auburn hair streaked with grey, she looked happy.

As D'arcy waved her lighter back and forth, Bonnie snapped a picture.

∿

After D'arcy returned to Canada, I revisited Père Lachaise several times, partly for respite from the constant hum of the city and partly to take advantage of this forty-eight hectare green space and sculpture garden to walk unrestrained by crowded sidewalks.

Paris cemeteries are not sad places. Workers on their lunch hours sit on benches eating meat-stuffed baguettes and sipping coffee; lovers stroll along the avenues, arms wrapped around each other; old men and women place fresh flowers in urns and sweep the leaves from family graves.

Before the mid-eighteenth century, Paris graveyards were close-ly associated with churches and religion. But after a rainy spring caused putrescent bodies from the cemetery at Les Innocents – in the area of Les Halles and the Pompidou Centre for modern art – to slide into the property next door, an edict banning all burials inside city limits was enacted. Over the next eighteen years, between six-and seven-million bodies were relocated to the catacombs, and Nicolas Frochot, under instructions from Napoleon Bonaparte, purchased land outside the city for new, secular cemeteries.[5]

When Père Lachaise first opened, Parisians didn't want to inter their dead in a rural and secular park-like setting. In the first year, only thirteen people were buried there.[6] Then Frochot devised a sure-fire marketing strategy that made it *the* place to be. He had the remains of Héloïse and Abelard, the Jim Morrisons of their time, transferred to the cemetery, and built an ornate tomb for the lovers' remains near the front gates.[7]

I stopped at their famous monument. I had heard of these lovers by way of Jean de Meung's *Roman de la Rose* when I studied Chau-cer, but until I saw their grave, I assumed they were fictional. When I looked them up, I learned that the story of Héloïse and Abelard, which has been called the greatest romance of all times, wasn't all that great.

Apparently, Abelard was a thirty-seven-year-old philosopher and teacher, and Héloïse, his brilliant nineteen-year-old student. Already, the story made the hairs on the back of my neck stand up. I knew where it was going. He seduced, she responded and the inevit-able happened. I could read their story almost a thousand years later because they corresponded with each other – she from a convent and he from a monastery – and their letters were discovered in the convent's library. If this is such a great love story, why weren't they together, I wondered. I was hooked.

I started to read *The Lost Love Letters of Héloïse and Abelard* – 113 fragments of letters believed to have been written while the lovers were courting – and I was overwhelmed by their honesty and boldness. In one, Héloïse says, "For I often come with parched throat longing to be refreshed by the nectar of your delightful mouth and to drink thirstily the riches scattered in your heart…There is no one in this world breathing life-giving air whom I desire to love more than you."[8] Abelard responds, "… I receive your letters so eagerly that for me they are always too brief, since they both satisfy and stimulate my desire: like someone who is suffering from fever – the more the drink relieves him, the hotter he feels."[9]

They were obviously hot for each other. But then, I can't help but feel Abelard took advantage of his student. Héloïse reacted to her pregnancy with joy.

Abelard writes about his reaction to the news and what happened as a result of it in a letter addressed to another monk. To console his friend Philintus (who had poured out all his woes to Abelard), the letter writer says, "Hear but the story of my misfortunes, and *yours*, Philintus, will be nothing."[10]

Abelard calls the unborn child a "burden" and writes, "The first news Héloïse acquainted me with plunged me into a thousand distractions."[11]

According to his letter, Abelard smuggled the pregnant Héloïse out of the city to his sister's house to avoid retribution from Héloïse's guardian and uncle – who also happened to be a canon at Notre Dame and Abelard's employer. When he asked her uncle's permission to marry, he did so without Héloïse's knowledge. Then Abelard demanded that the marriage be kept secret. To my mind, this was simply cowardice. He wanted it all: his job, his status as a brilliant scholar and a young wife. Her uncle wasn't happy, but he agreed.

I'd like to think there was a long and very loud debate when Abelard told Héloïse the plan. She was against marriage and later wrote, "I was very unwilling to be necessitated to love always a man who would perhaps not always love me. I despised the name of wife that I might live happy with that of mistress."[12] But as a young woman without means in the twelfth century, she had no control. She left her baby with Abelard's sister (who knows how willingly), returned to Paris, married Abelard in secret, and moved back with her uncle. Abelard lived by himself and continued to teach as if nothing had happened. They saw each other when they could meet, but only in secret.

When the relationship between Héloïse and her uncle soured (details about the type of abuse are not revealed), Abelard took his wife to a convent north of Paris. Her uncle, driven by revenge, organized a group of men who attacked and castrated Abelard.

Héloïse retired – not from a job but from the secular world.[13] And it wasn't easy for her. Fifteen years after Abelard forced her to take vows, she was an Abbess, but still she struggled with being a nun. "All who are about me admire my virtue, but could their eyes penetrate into my heart, what would they not discover? My passions there are in a rebellion; I preside over others, but cannot rule myself. I have but a false covering, and this seeming virtue is a real vice."[14]

For me, her story became a lesson in the power of "emotion regulation" – the ability to regain control by altering the way we see our lives. Héloïse took control by looking at her life in a different light. In one of her letters to Abelard, she suggests he do the same. "Govern yourself by my example. We have bound ourselves to severe austerities, and must follow them, let them cost us ever so dear. Let us think of our duties … and make a good use of that necessity which keeps us separate."[15]

She turned the Paraclete Abbey, where she was Abbess, into one of the most successful convents in France. She studied Latin, Greek and Hebrew and, according to historian John Hughes, was "esteemed a miracle of learning."[16]

Instead of the current tomb inscription, which speaks mostly of Abelard, I think visitors to the monument should be able to read the following: *Here lies Abelard, a teacher and scholar who didn't have the courage to publicly acknowledge his love for Héloïse. Here also lies Héloïse, his wife. She gathered together the fragments of her ruined life, wrested back control, reinvented herself and carried on.*

I wasn't prepared to go the prayer and convent route to send my retirement in a new direction, but I could certainly see how study might redirect my focus and jumpstart the next phase. Paris's history surrounded me, particularly in cemeteries. I set out to pursue stories in stone.

$\sim$

Even in the most romantic city in the world, there's always laundry. As I wrestled with the sheets and towels in our washing machine, I thought about Héloïse. I doubt she had to worry too much about such things. I have no way of knowing this for sure, since the letters don't speak of such mundane matters. But as her uncle was the canon of Notre Dame and she could read and write, her role in the convent was probably more intellectual than physical.

No matter how much I tried to control my immediate environment, I only occasionally mastered the apartment's washing machine. In order to save space, the owner had purchased an all-in-one washer/dryer and placed it under the counter in the kitchen. From day one, I had to lift the door into place. I couldn't wash anything on cold and once the machine had started, I couldn't figure out how to stop it to add something I had forgotten. Anyone who has used a European washer or dryer knows that each load takes twice as long as it does in a North American model. One afternoon, after D'arcy left, I loaded the machine with bedding, walked about two kilometres to a store I had read about that sold everything from dinnerware to pantyhose, then came back via the local green grocer. I must have been gone over two hours. When I opened the washer door the sheets were dripping wet. I have no idea what I had done differently that day. I tried rereading the instructions (*en français*) and studying the diagrams, but that didn't help. I bundled the sheets into a green garbage bag and took them to the laundromat, where, of course, all the directions were in French. A lovely young man helped me figure out how to pay. Too nervous to leave my load unguarded, I stayed.

There is nothing to do in a laundromat but read, and I had brought a copy of Alistaire Horne's *Seven Ages of Paris* to fill the time. As my sheets spun (for over an hour) I read Horne's chapter, "L'année terrible" about the siege of Paris and the Paris Commune.

~

On my last visit to Père Lachaise, about a week before we returned to Canada, I headed to a little-used pedestrian entrance. Stairs led underneath a four-metre stone wall, through a small gated arch at the end of rue de la Réunion. The entrance smelled of damp leaves, mold and urine; large pieces of stone were missing from the stringers, and orange caution tape made parts of the staircase inaccessible.

I had come to find the Mur des fédérées, the bullet-pocked wall that marked the massacre of 147 people, members of the Paris Commune. This left-wing group of artists, students, the working poor, former revolutionaries, feminists, socialists and anarchists were trying to bring an end to an imperial government and stimulate reforms for the poor and working class. In many ways, I was like them – a strong union supporter and a member of our teacher's status of women committee, fighting for equal treatment for both teachers and students. I demonstrated for a woman's right to choose and against our provincial government when our rights to same-sex benefits were denied. I can't drive through the intersection of Wellesley and Yonge Street in Toronto without wanting to stage a sit-in.

On September 1, 1870, having waged a war he could not win, Napoleon III surrendered to the Prussians and was taken prisoner. The provisional government that followed continued the war, even though it was costly and futile. In response, Bismarck's army besieged Paris for five months.[17] Poverty-stricken citizens starved; the wealthy ate fewer éclaires.

After the armistice, the former prime minister and now president of France sent his army up Montmartre to retrieve cannons used against the Prussians. The citizens of Montmartre believed those cannons belonged to them – so much so a mob defending the big guns attacked and killed two generals.[18] Terrified of the growing power of the working class, the government moved its seat from Paris to Versailles. A group from the left wing (many from the poorest areas of Paris, like Montmartre and Belleville) set up a rival government, the Paris Commune.

Women like Louise Michel, a trained teacher, were heavily involved with the Commune. Of course, women couldn't vote, but they were vocal about their beliefs and they attended meetings where their voices were heard. Michel wanted free schooling for all children (both boys and girls), childcare facilities, housing for the homeless and rights for prostitutes.

But like so many political parties, both then and now, the views of Commune members ranged from the far left to centre and while they agreed a new government was necessary, they disagreed on how to build it.

The Communards knew it wouldn't be long before the government's army would fight back. In March 1871, they did what their parents and grandparents did – they built barricades and armed themselves against the inevitable backlash. In April, a group of women formed the *Union des femmes pour la defense de Paris et les soins aux blesses* (Union of Women for the Defence of Paris and Aid to the Wounded) to support the fighters.[19]

The government's army attacked the city. The Communards fought back. Women like Michel helped at the barricades, supplying the men with food and caring for the injured. But by the end of May, the government's army regained the city and for eight days went on a killing spree.[20] On May 28, government troops marched 147 captured Communards to Père Lachaise where, avenging the murder of an archbishop, they lined up the Communards against the cemetery wall and shot them.[21]

Michel was not killed at that wall. After almost two years in a French prison, she was deported to New Caledonia. For me, those bullet holes were a stark reminder of the importance of standing up for our beliefs, but also of the risks we take when we confront big government and big money.

Like the Paris Communards, young Americans in 1970 were fed up with a war that had its roots in the '50s, escalated in the '60s and still had no convincing explanation. They wanted the government to pull out of Cambodia and Vietnam. As a teenager, I demonstrated against the war in Vietnam on more than one occasion – and that was in Canada. The draft and the number of young people killed in that war tore at my peace-loving, idealistic, folk-singing heart.

I was eighteen in 1970 when, on May 4, the National Guardsmen fired into a group of protesting students at Kent State University, killing four and wounding nine.

Unlike their French counterparts, the Kent State students were trying to bring about change through peaceful demonstration.

The killings at Kent State started nationwide strikes on college and university campuses, made politicians start to question America's role in Vietnam, and eventually led to the withdrawal of troops from Cambodia.

For the Paris Commune, the results weren't immediate. As Adam Gopnik points out in his *New Yorker* essay, "The Fires Of Paris," what the Communards fought for – more equality for workers, less involvement by the church – took fifty years to come to fruition "as France moved toward a modern welfare state, and firmly separated Church and nation."[22]

As I stepped up to the Mur des fédérées, I wondered what, if any, physical reminders were left from the Kent State shootings and whether, like me, people found themselves thinking about that day almost fifty years later. I found one of the bullet holes and pressed my thumb into the hollow. It fit perfectly. To my surprise, the indentation was smooth, not rough as I imagined it would be. How many other fingers had traced the wall's history, made a connection to the many who died there? I rested my forehead against the coolness of the north-facing wall and put my own puny troubles into perspective.

$\sim$

Leaving the wall, I felt a strange lightness. I didn't have to change the world, just *my* world. And that seemed more possible now as I examined what I could and couldn't control and tried to minimize my anxiety around the latter.

I thought back to Dalida and how, after so many changes in her life, she had run out of the energy or the will to do it again. Honouring her memory, I decided to try to find the grave of the man who had first discovered her: Bruno Coquatrix, owner of the 1950s Parisian music hall, Olympia.

But before that, I needed to find a washroom. Public toilets are marked clearly on each map, but just because they're on the plan, it doesn't mean they're open or usable. At the top of the stairs leading from the rue de la Réunion, boards and chains barred that toilet's door. When I got to the Gambetta entrance, a "Closed" sign hung on the washroom. The next-nearest facility I remembered was at the main entrance, a kilometre's hike away. I'm not a modest person and am not embarrassed to go behind a tree if I'm hiking. But I drew the line at sneaking behind some person's monument and doing the same. I set off in the direction of the front gate.

Fifteen minutes into my walk, I was reconsidering that vow. Then I heard someone marvelling at the size and cost of an elaborate monument – in English. She read the description aloud to her partner from her phone.

"Excuse me, do you happen to know where there's a washroom?"

"Turn left and walk a short way. It's a big building. You can't miss it. There's a washroom and some vending machines."

"Thanks." Strange, I thought. I didn't know about this facility, and as any one who knows me can attest, I know just about every public washroom anywhere I visit. Bonnie calls me "Princess Tiny Bladder."

I turned left, as instructed. Just as she described, a large building stood to my right – the crematorium. I stopped. It didn't feel right. But I was running out of options. After a painful walk past two outer walls containing niches for cremated remains, I found a door with a sign in French. "Entrance restricted to funeral participants." I walked around to the next door. Same sign. People gathered near the door and spilled onto the gravel drive. The women's saris were a collage of bright greens, royal blues and oranges. I couldn't intrude on their ceremony. Even if I wanted to, I could not walk in unnoticed. And that damn sign haunted me. After all, I am Canadian – and a wuss.

At the next entrance, I peered down the dim hallway. Visitors at a second funeral were just leaving. Luckily, I had worn a skirt and sweater and the mourners were dressed a little more like me. I put my camera into my purse, walked down the corridor, looking suitably somber, passed the officials, turned left at the hall with the sign for the *toilette*, and strode past the vending machines into the only stall.

Oddly, the woman who gave me directions hadn't said a word about the "Do Not Enter" signs. Maybe there were no funeral services in progress when her bladder sent her there. Maybe she couldn't read the French signs. Or, maybe, like me, she decided she just had to ignore them. Was I overly sensitive after my gaff at Montmartre? I wondered what a French tourist would have done in my situation? If I had been wearing jeans and garish running shoes, would one of the attendants have stopped me? All these thoughts, my guilt, plus the knowledge that there was only one toilet plagued me. *Relax, relax.* I finished, flushed and checked that my skirt wasn't tucked into my tights. I kept up a brisk pace back down the hall, ready with a Canadian "sorry" if required. My slowly rebuilding confidence, prompted by physical necessity, had brought out a stealthy interloper in my personality. I did it.

~

My defiance of rules at the crematorium may not have been a great demonstration of courage to some, but for me, it went against sixty years of ingrained rule-following. What happens if we never learn defiance, if we always follow rules and authority? How would France be different if those Communards had not fought for a fairer society? In desperate times, defiance is often the only logical response. It's blindly following rules that so often causes horrendous acts. Père Lachaise is filled with moving memorials to victims and heroes of the Holocaust. Although unspeakable acts were carried out by racist, sadistic bigots, many were committed by people who didn't think to challenge the rules. Reminders of this horrific period in France's history are scattered throughout Paris.

Three days before we returned to Canada, I found the Suzanne Buisson square just blocks from our apartment. It is dedicated to a sixty-year-old resistance fighter who sacrificed herself saving a friend from a Nazi ambush. She was one of many who every day defied the rules. Thrown into Montluc prison in Lyons, tortured, then deported, she died en route to a Nazi concentration camp.[23]

Hollywood depicts women in the resistance as young and, of course, beautiful. Influenced by these portrayals, I never pictured resistance fighters my age.

At sixty-one, I was only a year older than Buisson when she died. I felt ridiculously vulnerable disobeying signs in the Père Lachaise crematorium. I couldn't imagine the risks she faced every day and the courage she must have needed to continue. I wonder if, for her, resistance work was a way to seize power when everything felt out of her control.

Control was ripped from my father's grasp during the same war when a German U-boat sank the ship he was taking from England to New York City. Although he couldn't swim, he jumped overboard. When he hit the water, he discovered his inflatable life vest had a hole in it. He was pulled over the side of a lifeboat, where he spent the next eight days living on rations and black water, in constant fear of another U-boat attack. He wrote two or three sentences in his tiny pocket planner each day: "Sunday March 7: Night on board boat. Drifting with others. Surf howled. Mother boat towed others. Ours leaking badly. Transferred to mother boat. No room to sleep or stretch." These brief observations recorded in fountain pen were the only things he could control.

When Parkinson's disease robbed my dad of control over his body, he, like Suzanne Buisson, found something that gave him back a sense that he still had choices. At one point, he shared a hospital room with a young man in his twenties whose symptoms were already far worse than my dad's. When he came home, he kept talking about the age of the man and how unfair it all seemed. After that, my dad participated in one drug trial after another – two that almost killed him. Maybe this was his way of managing fear and uncertainty. That's bravery, the same kind of day-after-day courage shown by Buisson.

I honestly don't know if I have that same kind of bravery. The riskiest thing I've done is come out as gay. And that was in Canada in the last half of the twentieth century. From the Stonewall riots on, many had already fought on Bonnie's and my behalf. In the beginning, losing the children, our jobs and, of course, our rights to make life-and-death decisions about each other's healthcare were real threats. But I was never ostracized from my family or beaten for my life choices. I had gay and straight friends and family who loved and supported us. In retrospect, maybe retirement required more nerve.

Spending time with the dead helped me put my situation into perspective. To reconnect with the retirement I wanted, I had to train myself to embrace the unknown, step back and look at events more dispassionately – even pee with impunity. Like Héloïse, I had to grab control by not dwelling on the past and step bravely into my uncharted future – what was left of it. And like my dad and all the great freedom fighters, I needed to take risks, to explore my uncertainty and push the edges of my comfort zone.

As we packed our suitcases, I turned to Bonnie. "I think I want to go back to school."

CHAPTER 6

OLD DOG...NEW TRICKS: STEPPING INTO A NEW LIFE

This was *not* Paris. Tiered seats fanned out in a semicircle around an empty lecture hall. At the front of the room, a wooden lectern, a table and a blackboard stood clean and ready. I pulled my sweater tight around me, shifted my books to my right hip and thought back to my first day of university when I had waist-length brown hair, a homemade navy-blue pantsuit with stovepipe legs and a midi-vest edged with braid. Almost half a century later, the rock in the pit of my stomach – it's rough edges poking delicate tissue – felt much worse than it had all those years ago. What was I doing back at school?

I wondered if I had been temporarily insane when, energized and excited to get back to writing after Paris, I applied for this Masters of Fine Arts in Creative Non-fiction in Nova Scotia. How was school going to jumpstart the rest of my retirement?

My classmates included a semi-retired executive producer for a popular investigative show on CBC, a former "Facts and Arguments" editor at *The Globe and Mail*, as well as playwrights, poets and full-time, award-winning journalists. Their topics were hard core: missing and murdered Indigenous women, the threat to Canadian lakes by invasive carp, the dangers of the post-feminist age, and surviving the death of a child. Me? I wanted to write a literary travel book about Paris.

The term "imposter phenomenon" has been in use since 1978. It's a phenomenon experienced by high achievers who can't accept their success. I was a classic case.

The day I got my acceptance letter to the MFA program, I couldn't have been happier. But imposters can find many reasons for an accomplishment other than "I deserve it" or "I'm qualified." After the glow of my acceptance wore off, my doubts grew. I got accepted because:

- someone dropped out and they needed to fill the program;
- I was old and they wanted a range in ages and experiences;
- I was from the other side of the country and they needed a national distribution;
- I looked good on paper.

When we retire, we have lots of time to doubt ourselves. While the imposter phenomenon is destructive, it's also difficult to overcome because no one talks about it. One of the researchers who labelled this phenomenon, psychologist Dr. Suzanne Imes, says little can be done to change the imposter's feelings about herself. She is convinced she's the only one who feels this way and fears that if she told anyone else she was a phoney "she would meet with criticism or at least very little understanding on the part of others."[1]

Sadly, though not surprisingly, the tendency to believe we are frauds is more prevalent with women. Whereas men tend to put failure down to things beyond their control, women tend to blame themselves.[2]

It's funny. I never felt fraudulent when I was writing textbooks, teaching or helping other teachers, even when I earned promotions at work. My doubt seems strongest when I go to school. I've tried to pinpoint the reason for this. Was it because I always compared myself to my brother, who scored in the ninety-ninth percentile on the university entrance exams? Or maybe I couldn't forget my father's comment when I showed him my 88% in music: "What happened to the other 12%?"

Nonetheless, here I was. I found a seat in the third row from the front of the lecture hall. I hoped someone I knew would sit with me.

The hall was half full when Andrew arrived and sat beside me. I don't remember what we talked about – maybe invasive carp, the topic of his book. Or maybe he described his rooms off campus. What I do remember was how relaxed he seemed, like a master's program and writing a book were no big deal. In my twenties, school was so much easier because I knew everything; now, I knew so little.

Three hours of talking heads later, my brain felt like a cantaloupe that had been thrown from a moving car. Andrew rose from his seat, as nonplussed as when he sat down, said, "See ya," and left. I followed a group of my classmates through the maze of halls between the "new building" and the admin building, where I stood underneath the covered entrance, gathering myself together.

Across the quad, the white pillars on the semicircular portico of our residence, Alex Hall, rose two stories above the front steps. Not to be outdone, the four-columned entrance of the administrative building where I stood reached up three-and-a-half stories. The granite exteriors of both buildings added gravitas to the already serious Canadian neoclassical style and proclaimed, "This is a sober, staid university."

In contrast, the elegance and grace of the single-storey library's generous terrace and twelve-paned, nearly floor-to-ceiling windows beckoned. "Come in. Choose a book, snuggle up in a cosy corner and have some tea." I wanted to move in.

Instead, I returned to the dorm.

~

Choosing to live in student residence seemed romantic when I booked it. Our arrival into the city two nights earlier was fraught with drama. The flight from Vancouver to Toronto was delayed, forcing us to run through the airport to catch our next plane to Halifax, which landed just past midnight. Our luggage didn't arrive with us. By the time the taxi pulled into the residence, it was 2 in the morning. The young woman at the desk couldn't track down our reservation and finally put us in the only empty room she could find.

It was August. It was hot, and it was hellishly humid. We opened the window wide. A blanket of scorching wet air wrapped itself around the residence, stifling any possibility of a breeze.

About 4 in the morning, I got up to use the toilet across from our room. As I pulled open the bathroom door, a screech of metal on metal – like a slow-motion car crash – reverberated down the hall. Inside, trash cans overflowed with paper towels, and the sinks were veined with long, black hairs. When I finished in the toilet, I found the cleanest sink and washed my hands, all the while envisioning bacteria-infested floors and athlete's foot. Romance be damned. I vowed we'd rent rooms off campus next year, if I returned at all.

In the morning, we were both exhausted, but our luggage arrived and our new room was ready. The women's washroom was now down the hall, through two sets of double doors, as far away as one could get. At least we wouldn't hear the screeching metal in the middle of the night. The closest bathroom was labelled "Men." Even though I had infiltrated the restricted toilets in Père Lachaise's crematorium, I never disobeyed the sign in the residence.

The welcome barbeque was held the first evening at the Dalhousie University Club. Second-year students, relaxed and chatty, greeted each other like long-lost friends. I'm sure many spoke to me, though I don't remember who they were. The organizers quickly gathered us into our mentor groups, which saved me from feeling like I was at the grade seven social, standing against the wall hoping someone would ask me to dance. Our group – Suzanne, Jeff, Andrew (who sat with me the next day) and I – had already met on paper, having read each other's work in preparation for the course. Harry, our mentor, introduced himself and talked briefly about what we could expect in our time together. The first thing I noticed about him was how his eyes – they crinkled when he smiled – complemented his voice. There was a ring of laughter in his words. The second was his incredible head of curly hair. We stood by one of the square wooden pillars, sipping our drinks and sharing our arrival stories. Suzanne came from Antigonish, Andrew and his wife from

Toronto, Jeff from Newfoundland and Harry from about two hours outside Halifax.

In the meantime, Bonnie introduced herself to everyone in the pub, shared life stories and made bosom buddies with several people before the night ended. Unlike me, she has an ability to walk into a room full of strangers and seem completely at ease.

In her article, "Feel Like a Fraud?" Kirsten Weir suggests that being different from the majority of your peers can intensify feelings of fraud.[3] Although the average age in the course was around forty-two, I think I was the second eldest. I might have been the only retired person in my year. When we broke from our mentor groups, the younger crowd gravitated toward each other. I knew from the writing we had submitted before the course that Jeff's project centred on his experiences growing up gay in small-town Newfoundland. We talked a little longer before he too drifted off to join his age group.

I've always had trouble with names. When I taught, every semester I dreaded learning ninety new names. In the pub that first evening, after a serious forty-minute discussion with a woman, I had to say, "I'm sorry, what was your name again?" Please, don't ask me who she was. I can't remember.

Since then I've found a really good explanation for why we forget names. One theory suggests we store the sound of a person's name and the information associated with the name (hair style, clothing, eye glasses) in two different areas of the brain.[4] If we don't use the name often enough, the connection between the sound and information weakens and, while we might remember a face, we can't recall the name. Unfortunately, these connections also weaken with age, which is very bad news for someone like me.

The pub was hot and I had a hard time hearing over the buzz of conversation, bursts of laughter and clink of glasses at the bar behind me. The what-ifs started creeping in. What if I could no longer keep up with the work? What if my writing didn't measure up? Worse, what if I didn't fit in? It always comes down to that. I want to be accepted. When I was a teenager, I took up smoking to be part of a group. I wasn't about to take it up again.

I tried to recall the lessons I learned in Paris about quieting my busy brain, but sweat ran down my back and the beer sat uneasily in my stomach. I needed to go back to the residence, isolate myself in the shower and let the pounding water drown out my internal voices. Catching Bonnie's attention, I signalled, "Time to go."

∿

Thank God Bonnie came along with me to Halifax. After that first morning lecture when my head was packed and I was feeling out of my depth, I climbed the three flights of stairs in our dorm and let myself into our room. There were cold meats, cheese, fresh veggies, fruit and yogurt on plastic plates with plastic cutlery. The place smelled like a New York deli and felt like the Ritz.

But lunch was all too short. Ten minutes before the afternoon lecture, we assembled on the steps of the admin building for the official class photo. The first one is formal – everyone standing still, smiling at the camera. Looking at that picture now, I notice there are few people smiling. But I'm one of them. I hadn't seen this picture in over two years, and I'm shocked at how relaxed I looked.

The early part of the afternoon focused on preparing a book proposal. We all have selective memory – conveniently remembering some things and not others. I'm told the excruciating pain of childbirth is one of those things women forget. I forgot that school is hard – or maybe it's just harder now than it used to be. And there were marks involved. I'm an inveterate note-taker, but as my brain ages it is not as good as it used to be at suppressing distractions.[5] In the lecture I found it more difficult to identify salient information, remember it as I wrote and simultaneously listen for the next point. At the end of the one-and -a-half hours, I was exhausted. It's strange how something we never had to think about before becomes a challenge.

The final ninety minutes of that first day were set aside for pitches. In order to graduate, students had to produce a book-length manuscript with a view to publication, and each of us had to pitch and defend our book idea to the whole group. I was daunted by the complexity of the projects, and the slick presentations I saw that first day. Even on the hot seat fielding questions from mentors, the faculty supervisor and the executive director, my colleagues were cool and composed. The bar was set.

On day two, while our mentor group prepared our pitches, Harry told me in the gentlest way my book idea wasn't commercially viable – no publisher would want it. To help me come up with a new idea, he asked me about my trip to Paris, about the places I had been and about the stories I had discovered. He took notes on the board, connecting points with arrows. My classmates contributed ideas and helped me refine a new concept that excited me, one that Harry thought would work well.

I stayed up late labouring over my presentation. The next morning, I was wide awake by five. I got up, showered and sat in the little common room on the third floor. It was silent with sleep, and with that silence came calm. I worked until the floor awoke.

That afternoon as I entered the lecture hall, instead of jumping into catastrophic mode as I would have done in the past, I thought, "What's the worst that can happen?" I approached the lectern, called on my inner teacher and started into my eight-minute pitch. "It's an extraordinary story of two wealthy French families who collected art in the late nineteenth and early twentieth centuries. One was Protestant, one Jewish. One story ended in fame, the other in extermination." When I finished, the response was positive until one of the mentors asked, "Do you speak French?" As I answered "No," a splinter of doubt slid into my mind. But I still felt good. I had just delivered an idea that hadn't existed twenty-four hours earlier.

As the day wore on, that splinter worked its way deeper and deeper. I read French so slowly, I would have to live full-time in Paris's libraries and archives to review the literature. And what about interviews? I couldn't afford to pay an interpreter to accompany me. It was a good project, but the research alone would take longer than the course – maybe longer than the time I had left on this earth.

I knew the program directors wanted to shepherd as many projects as possible through to publication – a goal they supported with opportunities most writers never get. We would work on chapters, pitches and proposals guided by our mentors. During publishers' week – the first year in New York and the second in Toronto – we'd meet and pitch to editors, agents and marketing managers. But the project for this course would take two years of my life and, although I had just started, I knew it would define who I was for those years and maybe beyond. Retired, I could devote as much time as I wanted to my course work. And knowing me, I would spend many more hours than expected. Projecting a false identity – at any time in life, including retirement – is stressful and exhausting, says Kenneth Shultz (*Happy Retirement: The Psychology of Reinvention*). One reason I went back to school was to help me find out who I was outside my role as a teacher. If I pursued this new story, would it be like wearing another person's clothes for two years in order to fit the university's definition of success, not mine?

I met Suzanne and Jeff on the steps of the admin building after class and, with trembling bottom lip, asked, "Do you have a few minutes?" We huddled together at the bottom of the stairs.

"I think I have to go back to my original idea."

I'm not sure exactly what they said, but this is how I remember it. Suzanne tipped her head to the side. It's something she did when she was paying attention. I trusted her opinion. In class, her observations were always incisive and erudite. "It's a good idea. Look at the galleries you've included, and the art. People will be fascinated with the stories you've found."

"I know I can't do the story I pitched. It would take too long. But I'm afraid the program directors will have a problem with that. Then I'll have to decide whether or not to continue."

"You need to write what you want," Jeff said. "They're not going to fail you if you fulfill the course requirements." He was fighting his own battles, not with a school administration but with his body. Not long before the course started he had undergone his final round of chemotherapy for testicular cancer. Each day, he struggled to find the energy for classes and homework assignments. Yet he took time to listen, to commiserate and to encourage me.

I was most nervous about the impact my decision would have on Harry. Like me, he was going through this program for the first time. I didn't want my stubbornness to reflect badly on him. But I was taking Kenneth Shultz's advice to heart: publishing commercially had become less important to me than the intrinsic value of writing. There were many avenues for self-publication if I wanted to pursue them. Schultz says, "It's counter-productive to 'tidy up' the self; better to accept identity's intrinsic messiness and resistance to neat formulations." [6] My determination to return to my original idea felt messy, but also felt true to me.

Over a dinner meeting with Harry, I explained my decision.

"Do what you think is best. Let's work with it," he said. The needle on my anxiety meter – at "extreme" when I arrived at the restaurant – dropped to calm-*ish*.

∿

While I was in classes, Bonnie filled her time the best she could; however, without a car she was limited to walking in the extreme heat or drinking coffee and sketching in the air-conditioned Coburg Coffee House. A third option presented itself on Friday of the first week. An inveterate reader, she went into the university library and found a book about a French painter and artist's model working at the time of the Impressionists. Our class had had difficulties getting student cards, so Bonnie told the librarian about the delay, said she was Suzanne Harper and gave my student number. The librarian was happy to check out her book. I would never have thought to try, but Bonnie has a history with libraries. When she was a child, she used other kids' cards when she had too many books out on her own. While she had no scruples about using my card, I was convinced I would be kicked out of the university before finishing the residency.

She shrugged. "It's not a problem." When she returned the book on Monday afternoon, however, the librarian asked to scan her student card so the book could be entered back into the system. "I'll come back," Bonnie said. By that time I had picked up my student

ID – I was so proud of that card – and with great trepidation, I hand-ed it over to her. Bonnie is five-foot-eight and freckled with sandy hair. I'm five-foot-four with titanium-white hair. Bonnie predicted they wouldn't examine the card. To my shock and relief, they didn't. Expulsion averted – for now.

∽

The delay getting our student cards was one of many small glitches. Our MFA program was only in its second year and the course dir-ectors were still working out content. I think "more is better" might have been their motto. Lectures, seminars, presentations, one-on-one meetings and assignments filled our days; however, according to the second-year students, we had it easy. Sometimes talking to them, I felt like I had walked into a Monty Python skit. "You think you have it bad? We had to wake up two hours before we went to bed, and write a book a day with a quill pen."

As a teacher who has designed many new courses, I recognized the "oops-we-hadn't-thought-of-that" reaction when things didn't go as planned. The faculty supervisor contradicted messages delivered by the executive director. Assignments were modified midstream. Due dates were changed. While this "flexibility" didn't bother me too much (my aging amygdala kicking in?), it was anathema to some of the younger students who saw university courses, especially at the Master's level as fixed. One young man labelled the course the "DIY MFA." Except when it meant doing work that was later deemed unnecessary, I found the rethinking and reconstructing refreshing. Most university courses have been taught the same way for so long, reading lists are laminated and lecturer's notes might as well be too. There's an energy and excitement in the initial years that can't be replicated when courses become established.

But I said nothing. I was content sitting in lectures and taking notes, and while I had connected with people in my mentor group, I hadn't bonded with anyone else. Occasionally, during breaks, I sat on the steps of the admin building with the smokers, a mixed group of first- and second-year students and mentors. Fragments of those conversations float through my memory. "I don't think I can get up there in front of all those people…And there are mice in the kitchen…You don't have homework? We have writing assignments every night…I miss the kids…Have you been to the farmers' market?" Evenings, I was too tired to go to the pub, and Bonnie and I ate lunch and dinner together either in the residence or downtown.

Chatting over a meal with one of the older second-year students during publishers' week in New York, I discovered my feelings of isolation weren't unique. Deirdre was about my age, a former English teacher and freelance writer who had worked in Canada, England and Kenya. Her project focused on the life of Lily Jamon, a milliner who designed hats in the '50s and '60s for prime ministers' wives as well as for the Stratford Festival in Ontario. Deirdre had knowledge and experience, yet she also felt outside the group.

The point at which we feel irrelevant in the eyes of the younger generation has been labelled "the changing of the generational guard."[7] This sudden change in status can make us feel useless, can contribute to that post-retirement crash many of us experience. While at work, we might have been sage mentors, the people less-experienced employees sought out for advice or for a solution to problem. That all disappears when we quit work.

According to retirement experts, volunteering can help us make the transition from centre of the universe to orbiting satellite. When we use the skills we've learned to help guide the younger generation, we can still feel valuable. If any of my classmates had wanted to teach, I could have given them great advice on course planning and teaching techniques. But what guidance could I offer on a program we were all taking for the first time? Grad school had changed. I finished my master's degree in English before the invention of disposable contact lenses, digital cell phones and the Internet.

Many of the students in my year already had degrees in journalism. I didn't. They had more to teach me than I did them. They were either surviving or flourishing as writers under the most difficult conditions. For thirty-one years, I had a full-time job, a permanent position with benefits. As soon as I tried to freelance, I caved.

While some of my classmates already held responsible positions as magazine editors and reporters, many worked on contract. These young (and not so young) students were blogging, Facebooking, Tweeting, Pinning, YouTubing, Snapchatting and probably using ten other types of social media I hadn't heard of to get themselves known. They were publishing wherever they could, however they could, paid and unpaid. They were amazing. Sadly, few of the graduates from our course are likely to get tenured positions at universities, but I predict many will publish books to great acclaim.

Of course, I loathe becoming irrelevant. But I know I have to. We can't have old folks running the world. When I think about my classmates, their entrepreneurial spirit, their hard work, their drive, I feel less distressed about them taking over the universe and more content to be a satellite.

Looking back, I wish I had attended more social gatherings and made more of an effort to seek out their wisdom during breaks and after classes.

$\sim$

Over the two-week residency, four evenings were set aside for micro-readings, a chance for us to practice presenting our work in public. Having taught creative writing in high school, I've read my writing aloud many times. Still, I signed up for the last possible night, the Wednesday of the second week. I chose an excerpt from a piece I had written on the unpredictability of Paris, which had received positive comments when I read it in my mentor group.

The reading was held in the basement of the administrative building in a grotty room that served as a cafeteria by day, bar at night. It smelled like athletic socks, worn too many times and left to marinate in a gym bag. The poor acoustics were further hampered by the open bar, where staff banged glasses around and talked over each other. Adversity often brings people together. For the first time, I felt part of my class. Those who had read on other evenings at the University Club pub knew how nerve-wracking the experience could be under ideal conditions and rallied around. Those of us who were reading that evening stood together talking anxiously about the noise level in the room, whether or not to use a microphone and the pros and cons of reading from paper versus screen.

When my turn came, I put on my teacher voice (a slightly lower tone with much less breath) and started. Although I wanted to rush, I measured my words, looked up at the audience during dramatic pauses and kept an even pace to the end. The room burst into applause. After, people from both years congratulated me.

It had taken a week and a half, but I finally felt like I was where I should be. My trepidation about belonging, and my feelings of fraud, had kept my protective walls high and impenetrable. But over the final three days, things changed. We had dinner out with another couple in the course. Between classes I had long chats with students in other mentor groups, comparing what we had done in our various classes. I participated more confidently in conversations with the smokers on the admin building steps – I didn't seem to be invisible any more. I even managed several random get-togethers with students in both first and second year.

The second-last day of classes, I lost my pen. No big deal, you might be thinking, but this was a left-handed Pelikan fountain pen I had used for the roughs of everything I had published. I know I was far too attached to it, but its loss felt like a very bad omen. I went into my mentor group. "Has anyone seen my red fountain pen?" No one had. I searched the lecture hall, looked under the desks in the classrooms we had used. Nothing.

The next morning, Andrew asked if I had found my pen. I thought it was sweet he remembered. He was a young man with an old soul.

"Thanks for asking. No. And I'm devastated. I've had it for so long." Then I paused and with a tone of resignation and despondency said, "I guess I'll have to get a new one in Paris."

Andrew looked at me with a weird half-frown, half-smile on his face. "You know, Sue, no one is going to feel sorry for you if you add 'in Paris' to the end of your sentence, no matter how sad you are."

When I arrived back from class on the final day, Bonnie presented me with an 2.5 m. long calendar she had drawn without a ruler on four sheets of newsprint taped together. She had been accepted to two more art courses, and we were flying to Paris the following day. Henri Matisse once said creativity takes courage. I hoped I had Matisse's courage. At that moment it was all potential, a blank canvas. That evening I started to fill in due dates and tried to imagine what it was going to be like to write in the City of Light.

CHAPTER 7

PERSEPHONE UPENDED: MYTH BUSTING

Our second apartment in Montmartre was about 25 sq. m., roughly one-quarter the size of the tired but spacious place we lived in during the winter of 2013. I'm pretty sure the kitchen didn't meet any existing building codes. The electric stovetop sat directly beside the sink; I used it for a drying rack. But it was inexpensive and, as Andrew said, *we were in Paris*. Our front door faced rue Ravignan, the street that just about killed me in the snow eighteen months earlier. There was no chance of snow this time. It was fall. Three days after we arrived, Bonnie left Paris for a painting course held just south of the Loire Valley in a tiny village called Argenton-les-Vallées. She'd return to Paris in six weeks for another drawing course. I was on my own. But coping with daily life – the shopping, the laundry (we were close to the same laundromat so I knew how to select the machine I was using and how much to insert into the pay machine), getting around on the métro and trusting my mapping brain a bit more – was all much less intimidating.

Chestnuts fell in place Émile Goudeau. Their green husks split, exposing the shiny brown nuts inside. They reminded me of a game called "conkers" we played as children. It was a back-to-school game, a competition to crack our friends' chestnuts with our own.

I didn't often win that game – I had terrible aim, I wasn't adept at finding the hardest chestnuts and my unskilled drilling always made the hole too large – but I loved to play. The specimens in place Émile Goudeau were perfect weapons. I was tempted, but I had neither drill nor foe. The one foe I battled daily lived inside me, the insidious imposter residing in Paris who had a datebook filled with deadlines and people on the other side of the Atlantic waiting to critique academic reports and drafts of chapters.

Horse chestnuts say winter is coming. There were fewer people sitting in the square, mornings were chilly and brown leaves crackled underfoot. Soon, Le Relais de la Butte, a Montmartre restaurant founded in 1672, would reduce the number of outdoor tables and chairs. The square would take on the skeletal beauty of barren trees, silent fountains and empty park benches. And there would be rain. It would be the way I saw it when we arrived that first winter.

School work gave my life structure, and the predictability, the inevitability of structure has a way of calming me down. I taped my homemade calendar on the wall in our tiny salon. Each day, I recorded the number of hours spent researching, writing and completing academic assignments. Even if I really screwed up, the notes on this calendar proved I had worked hard.

As I wrote in the mornings, I could hear the family next door getting ready for the day. There were two children. For the first two weeks, the youngest, a little boy, screamed when he got up, screamed when he went down the stairs with his mom to daycare and then screamed into the evening when they arrived home. In the third week, he replaced crying with singing. He sang when he got up, sang when he went down the stairs with his mom and then sang into the evening when they arrived home. I wrote; he serenaded. *"Frère Jacques, Frère Jacques, dormez-vous? Dormez-vous? Sonnez les matines, sonnez les matines."* He also liked "Happy Birthday."

I thought about that little boy growing up, going to school, becoming a teenager. It occurred to me that, when he turned twenty, I may not be alive. The idea didn't depress me, just made me reflect on what a privileged life I led, to be able to go back to school and to be in Paris. With that feeling of privilege came a feeling of guilt. Not everyone had the same opportunity. I'd better not fuck it up.

With Bonnie away, my mornings followed a pattern. Set my alarm for forty minutes and work; do several yoga stretches when my sciatic nerve flared up; set my alarm for forty minutes, work; do more yoga stretches, brush my teeth; set my alarm, go back to my writing...until my work hours totalled three. I rarely wrote in the afternoon. I was working on a literary travel book and I couldn't do that without seeing more and learning more about Paris than I had the last time. What a change from that first trip when, for the first couple of weeks, all I wanted was to be cocooned, safe inside four walls.

By Friday morning of the second week, I decided *to hell with my routine.* My brain was exploding and if my calendar was blank for that day, I'd just have to deal with it. I picked up a *pain au chocolat* at Le Coquelicot, hopped on the métro and set off across Paris for Montparnasse cemetery, a cemetery I had previously neglected.

An overcast sky gave rise to the diffuse light photographers wish for when taking outdoor shots. The scatter of yellow and orange leaves between graves, and the red coat on a little girl holding her mother's hand, were as intense as if someone had pumped them up in Photoshop. The trees scrubbed the city air clean, and my long trench coat and scarf kept off the chill.

Autumn is a paradox. In literature, it represents ripeness, maturity, wisdom, but also a decline toward winter and death. In fall, according to Greek mythology, Persephone prepares for her return to the underworld. Trees lose their leaves, plants die and the earth is barren.

But because, in Canada, we start school in autumn, for me, it has always been a season full of possibilities. I had forty-nine school starts, thirty-one of them as a teacher. Each September, I fantasized about how I would change my students' lives forever and pictured a former student thanking me as he or she accepted the Nobel Prize for Literature. I probably thought about that because I was standing in front of Samuel Beckett's unassuming black-granite slab. He was most famous for writing the absurdist play, *Waiting for Godot,* a play often taught in high school, which, I'm embarrassed to say, I never liked and never taught. But he did win the Nobel Prize. After each September's honeymoon period ended, reality hit. Not all my students were exceptional, and I didn't have teaching superpowers.

Even now, I miss the anticipation of starting school. In my family, new shoes were part of our back-to-school ritual. I looked down at my shoes, purchased before leaving for Paris. Faux Mary Janes, they were leather with a strap across the instep, and round toes, a nod to the shoes I wore as a child and not too dissimilar to the red shoes worn by the woman who found the Louvre "unimpressive." Comfortable school shoes would be a good way to describe them. I envy women who can wear fashionable pumps like the ones I saw in Sylvie's Souliers across from the métro station on rue des Abbesses. They had heels right out of Marie Antoinette's court, about five centimetres high, shaped like an hourglass. Purple, moss green, even yellow, they tied with satin ribbons across the instep. I coveted those shoes, until I imagined the bunion on my right foot screaming under the pressure and my ankle turning over as my heel slipped off a cobblestone. Only a woman in the autumn of life would consider safety before style.

Still imagining myself in those shoes, I took a last look at Beckett's grave before continuing my walk. According to A&E's biography site, Beckett didn't attend the ceremony for his 1969 Nobel Prize.[1] If he had, would he have thanked any of his teachers in his speech? As I strolled further into the cemetery, I realized seven years had passed since my retirement. I thought about how much better I felt about myself almost two years after that first winter in Paris. I had purpose. I was more confident – I was even walking through this cemetery without a map. That would not have happened my first year. I had this new direction; now I had to do something about it.

When I left Halifax, one part of the pitch I made to my class followed me onto the plane and back to Paris. Although I couldn't write a book about Moïse de Camondo, the Jewish banker and art collector whose home became a museum, something about his story grabbed me and wouldn't let go.

When I first visited Musée Nissim de Camondo (named after de Camondo's son, Nissim), it was a cold, rainy winter day and I was somewhat reluctant. It had been recommended by one of Bonnie's art-course friends. I'm not a fan of Decorative Arts – furnishings, rugs and porcelain – but I love snooping in other peoples' homes, and this museum was located in one of the grand *hôtels particuliers* (private homes of the rich and famous).

I expected a *belle époque* house with a Second Empire roof (flat on the top with the shingles covering the sides of the top floor and then flaring out). It's the architecture that most of us think of as "typical" Paris. That I even knew this style is what comes of living with an artist. But then I thought perhaps de Camondo might have been influenced by Charles Garnier, who built the extravagant Garnier Opera House with its lavish columns, arches and gold. I was wrong on both counts. Although de Camondo built his house around 1911, it looked like a throwback to pre-French Revolution eighteenth century.[2] It was like a little Versailles. While Gustave Eiffel had erected his tower and Hector Guimard had designed the incredibly sensuous Art Nouveau entrances to the métro, whoever was responsible for this place was stuck in some other era. Later, I found out de Camondo had modelled it on the Petit Trianon, a house built at Versailles in the 1760s and given to Marie Antoinette by her husband, the king.

Inside, there were vases from the court of Marie Antoinette, ornate clocks, paintings by Élisabeth Vigée Le Brun (Marie Antoinette's favourite painter), Gobelin rugs and priceless Aubusson tapestries. The shoes I coveted would have felt very much at home in this place.

The longer I stayed, the more uncomfortable I felt. Moïse de Camondo's collection went beyond an homage to an age; it was a re-creation, a movie set, a shrine to a French social class into which he, as a Jewish man, would never have been welcomed. And yet he saw this era as the pinnacle of the French at their artistic best. What made it worse for me was knowing that his daughter, son-in-law and two grandchildren would be dead within a decade of him donating his collection – killed by the same kind of prejudice and bigotry that characterized the era he loved.

I stood in the kitchen, the only place other than the bathrooms where modernity crept into the home. Was this priceless art collection of French artists de Camondo's way of trying to fit into the French upper-crust society? To be almost more French than the French? In my original pitch back in Halifax, I said I was going to compare him to the Jacquemart-Andrés, a wealthy Protestant banking family. They too started collecting eighteenth-century French art, but then sold most of it to purchase Italian and Dutch masters. What gave me the idea to compare these two families in the first place was the audioguide in the de Camondo museum. The narrator said de Camondo was pissed off (OK, he didn't use those exact words) that the Jacquemart-Andrés were abandoning their collection. He saw them as sort of traitors to French art.

As I was on the subway coming home from my day at the Montparnasse cemetery, I thought about de Camondo's need to fit in to French society and wondered how much my obsession with wanting to know more about him and his family had to do with my own need to fit in to the program at Kings with all its serious researchers and writers.

CHAPTER 8

WALKING BESIDE THE MARTYRS: THE TRIALS OF VENTURING FORTH

Young men, dressed in flak jackets and carrying machine guns, patrolled the entrance to the Shoah Memorial when I approached on that cool, late-September morning. In Hebrew, *shoah* means "catastrophe." It's the term used in France (and many other places) for what we in Canada call the Holocaust.

Following Israel's bombing of Gaza during the summer of 2013, anti-semitism in France – not just from the Muslim community – was once again on the rise. Part of me said I was probably in the safest place in the city. The other part – the one that projected calamity – imagined hooded thugs subduing the guards and taking staff and visitors hostage. I seriously considered going back to the apartment, but then thought about the thousands of people whose courage outweighed their fear, who wouldn't give in to the Nazi murderers.

A guard behind thick bulletproof glass buzzed me into the security area. My bag went through the metal scanner and I walked through to the plaza. There were no windows overlooking the court-yard, just a blind wall with a large Star of David and two inscriptions. The French one read, "Before the Unknown Jewish Martyr, bow your head in piety and respect for all the martyrs. Walk beside them in your thoughts on their long, painful road. It will lead you to the highest summit of justice and truth."

I turned and stepped down to the wall of names. I felt over-whelmed by the narrowness of the pathway between the three-metre high walls engraved with each victim's name and date of birth. I walked beside 76,000 Jews deported from France. I walked beside Moïse de Camondo's son-in-law, Léon Reinach, and his grandchil-dren, Fanny and Bertrand. I walked beside his daughter, Béatrice de Camondo. I wanted to imagine their road, wanted to trace their journey. The de Camondo museum would be part of my literary travel book and now, so would the Shoah Memorial.

∽

But I need to step back, to explain my own journey, the path the de Camondo family led me down. I didn't think I could do justice to the museum without knowing more about the family, more than just seeing their names on a plaque inside the museum entrance, more than the information available from the Internet or on the audioguide.

I had three-and-a-half months in Paris, plenty of time to work on my academic assignments, visit new sites and delve further into the de Camondo family's history. Moïse de Camondo may have been a wealthy banker, but he suffered personal losses that money couldn't fix. When his youngest child, Béatrice, was three, his wife left the family for their horse trainer. De Camondo's oldest child, Nissim, died in World War I fighting for France. The grand house and art collection that would have gone to Nissim on his father's death were bequeathed to France in Nissim's name.

Béatrice became a secondary character in the de Camondo story and her mother, Irène, a mere walk-on. I'm one of those old-time 1970s feminists and the de Camondo story seemed to centre on the males. What about Irène? What was Béatrice like, growing up the daughter of divorced parents? What was her relationship with her father and her brother? Did she have contact with her mother? What kind of marriage did she have and why were she and her family arrested and deported?

Unlike Dalida, whose story got me out into the streets of Paris, tracing the de Camondo's and specifically Béatrice's path drove me indoors. I went first to the National Library of France – (Bibliothèque Nationale de France or BNF) – François Mitterrand Site, where my increased self-assurance and perseverance were tested.

If it weren't for Adam Gopnik, I wouldn't have known about the library. My first winter in the city, I read *Paris to the Moon,* a collection of personal essays he wrote over the five years he, his wife and son lived in Paris. Gopnik's description of the library's architecture – the steep stairs leading to a plaza that reminded him of the "pyramids where Aztecs plucked the hearts out of their sacrificial victims"– and the overwhelming bureaucracy of the place made me laugh out loud.[1] On rereading those passages prior to going there, however, the story wasn't quite as funny; in fact, it was frightening. I fervently hoped Gopnik leaned toward hyperbole.

I approached the library entrance from a different direction than Gopnik had, thus missing the plaza, but I did feel the full force of the wind-tunnel effect he described. As I picked my way down a flight of wet, slippery metal stairs to the entrance, the wind whipped up from the courtyard below and blew my umbrella inside out, almost knocking me off my feet.

Past the security check, I stalled for time, intimidated. Gopnik had warned of the staff's "functional hospitality." [2] To pluck up my courage, I walked the length of the glass-fronted main hall, checked out the two-stalled washroom, browsed in the bookstore and stared at the coat check where people were getting little see-through plastic briefcases and transferring everything from their backpacks into them. Past the coat check, two turnstiles and two immense metal doors kept the riff-raff out of the reading rooms.

Gopnik is fluent in French. He could bypass the help desk. I, on the other hand, waited in line to speak to Vincent, a serious, bespectacled young man. I was prepared for the "Who are you; what do you want; what makes you think...?" grilling to come.[3] My King's University student card, a COLL card – supposedly recognized internationally by institutes of learning – and the reference number of a book on the de Camondo family from the library's collection were tucked securely into a pocket in my purse.

I was feeling a bit more confident about my ability to speak. I studied French in university, but that was forty-five years earlier. It was hard to remember vocabulary let alone the complexities of reflexive verbs and indirect objects. So, after returning from my first winter in Paris, I read *Le Monde* online, attended a couple of evenings of conversational French organized by a friend of mine and, in New Zealand, did a language exchange with a young woman from France who wanted to improve her English.

Thomas Bak, a researcher for a study out of Edinburgh University, suggests learning a language later in life might be better than learning it earlier because it takes more effort.[4] I'm not so sure. He claims effort helps maintain the brain's neuroplasticity – its ability to reconfigure itself in response to new experiences. Trying to improve my French seemed to get harder and harder as I came face to face with everything I didn't know and promptly forgot something I had just learned.

As I sat down, my resolve to encourage more nimble neurons crumbled. Brain exercise be damned. I didn't have the vocabulary or the confidence to explain my research needs, and I really wanted a library card. Thankfully, Vincent spoke English.

"All applicants must prove to the librarians their need to research." He pointed to a row of serious-looking men and women sitting at desks, separated from the main flow of human traffic by stanchions strung together with retractable nylon belts. "What are you working on?" I showed him my student card and the book reference, and explained what I was looking for. He nodded his approval. "Good. You will need to undergo an admissions interview. Simply describe the nature of your research. Most of the librarians speak English. They will take your photograph and issue your card."

Vincent directed me to the admissions desk. The librarian (I'll call him Jacques) did not speak English. I pulled my student ID and the reference number for Pierre Assouline's *Le dernier des Camondo* from my purse. Every time he asked me a question, I made him repeat it at least twice. When he inquired about my research, I summarized as best I could. Either he understood what I wanted, or thought it easier to grant me a card than not.

The camera on his computer failed four times before he turned me over to his colleague, the sort of woman Gopnik describes as "severely disciplinary."[5] I couldn't understand a word she said. Was I supposed to sit? Move the chair back? Tilt my head? By the time my photo was taken, my face was stuck in a permanent rictus.

I walked out of the library that day with a fifteen-day reader's card, forty-five euros (about $68 Canadian) poorer. I had not touched a book. My nerves were so jangled, I went immediately to Bon Marché, a huge department store that sells products from around the world, and spent five euros (about $8 Canadian) on a miniscule jar of peanut butter. Comfort food.

Rereading Gopnik's description of the lower floors of the library, I prepared myself for the ten-storey escalator, the concrete walls, the trees chained to the ground in the submerged forest and the huge, cheerless reading rooms.

My book took over thirty minutes to arrive, which gave me plenty of time to think back over the past eighteen months – my first time exploring a city by myself, getting accepted to grad school, travelling across the country for a summer residency and now, perhaps the biggest accomplishment, defeating the many heads of the French bureaucratic Hydra to get my BNF library card. I sat up a little straighter in the hard, wooden, straight-backed chair and mentally puffed out my chest. Eighteen months earlier I wouldn't have needed an Aztec to throw me off the pyramid. I would have done it myself.

Then I thought about the de Camondo book making its way from one of the glass towers to the librarian's desk. Would I be able to read it? Was I wasting my time pursuing something that wasn't going to be a major part of my manuscript?

When the librarian handed me the small, apparently never-opened paperback, I studied the sepia-toned cover photo of Moïse de Camondo sitting in a wicker garden chair. He's wearing a suit, complete with a vest, and a straw boater. Beside him sits his son, Nissim, legs crossed, looking relaxed in his dress uniform. Once again, the men took centre stage. Even the title, *The Last of the Camondos*, suggested the author would focus on the Camondo line, which excluded the daughter, Béatrice. I hoped she figured in the story somewhere.

As I started to read – very slowly – a man beside me snorted and huffed so loudly, translating became impossible. Then the sun came through the high clerestory windows and with it, extreme heat. I was done. I couldn't check out the book, so carefully replaced it on the cart under a sign that said to do so, and left. Ten minutes later, when my card wouldn't activate the exit turnstile, I discovered I was supposed to return the book to the checkout desk. I ran back to the reading room, retrieved the book from the cart (thanking the Goddess of aging unilingual brains – I'll call her Confusia) and returned it to the librarian, who swiped my card.

The next day, I went to a Gibert Joseph bookstore and found the same edition in exactly the same condition for seven euros, ninety-five (roughly $12 Canadian).

Bonnie was still in rural France, which meant my time was my own. Nights, I'd sit in bed, my French/English dictionary beside me and the window open onto the internal courtyard, where pots and pans rattling in sinks and snatches of French conversation became the background to my reading.

As I learned about the characters in the de Camondo tragedy, I came across a story I remembered from my visit to the museum. Irène Cahen d'Anvers, the ex-wife who ran off with the horse trainer, had been painted when she was a child by the famous Impressionist, Auguste Renoir. I immediately found the picture online. She's about eight years old. She sits in profile, her head turned just slightly toward the artist. Her hair cascades down her back and over her shoulders to her waist. The blue bow in her hair matches her blue-and-white dress. It's a beautiful portrait, now part of the Buehrle collection in Zurich. (Could Bonnie be convinced to take a little side trip to Zurich when her studies finished?)

I was prepared to dislike Irène. But I admit she had guts. She left a comfortable home and two children under ten to follow her heart. She could have stayed with Moïse and kept a lover on the side, as many women did in that era, including her mother.[6] After her separation, Irène had regular visits with Béatrice and Nissim until she converted to Catholicism in order to marry Charles Sampieri – the horse trainer and erstwhile count – and became Countess Sampieri. After the marriage, she lost that access to her children.[7]

When Bonnie and I met, we were both married to men. Imagine our surprise when we fell in love. We decided to move in together, but we risked losing her two daughters. Our lawyer warned us we could never tell anyone we were a couple, that the courts would rather give the children to an axe murderer than lesbians. We were willing to take that risk but lived as discreetly as possible (maintaining the appearance of roommates) until our society's views and the laws changed. Unlike Irène, we kept the girls. But I identified with Irène's situation.

Some might argue she was foolish, but I think Irène was brave. Her father disinherited her.[8] She was forced to return the Renoir painting, which had been given to her as a wedding present. In that portrait she is looking off into the distance, a little bit wistful or maybe contemplative. The child in the painting certainly wasn't imagining a future so difficult.

The de Camondo children must have had an interesting upbringing and yet little of this was reflected in the museum or in Pierre Assouline's book.

At school, I listened to my classmates talk about how they got sources for stories they were chasing. They called and wrote and accosted people on the street to get information. Sometimes they got turned down; sometimes they made amazing contacts. I wanted to get into the de Camondo museum archives. I thought the chances were slim and, in the past, rejection had sent my self-confidence into a tailspin. But I wasn't satisfied relying on book research. I had to get up the courage to ask for permission to work in the Musée Nissim de Camondo archives and accept whatever happened.

I made an email request – in English – to Les Arts Décoratifs, the non-profit organization responsible for the museum. It took a full month for the assistant curator to reply. She wrote back in French asking me to be more specific about my request, but sometimes I don't know what I'm looking for until I find it. What I really wanted was to rummage through the artifacts as if the archives were an antique store or garage sale, but I knew that wouldn't fly. I responded (in French, assisted by Google Translate) with several questions about the family, including Nissim and Béatrice's relationship with each other and with their father and mother, and Béatrice's life after her marriage and before the occupation. I was a little surprised when she agreed. We arranged a rendezvous for a day the museum was closed.

I arrived at the front gate. My heart pounded as I stood on the street, my finger hovering over the bell for the museum's interphone. Visions of the King's lecture hall and the question period following my book pitch haunted me. "Do you speak French?" "How will you conduct interviews?"

I pressed the buzzer. A disembodied voice crackled through the speaker. I *think* it said something to the effect that the museum was closed. In rehearsed but halting French I explained I had a rendezvous with Mme le Tarnec. Someone buzzed me through the fortress gates. I was met by a cleaner, who handed me off to another woman, who escorted me to the top floor and into the curator's office. I think it was lined floor to ceiling with bookshelves, and there might have been a carpet on the floor. I remember her desk being large, but I couldn't describe it. My head was spinning and my heart thudded in anticipation.

Although our correspondence had been in French, I hoped le Tarnec spoke some English. She had co-authored one of the definitive books on the de Camondo family and probably dealt with scholars from around the world in her position as curator.

"*Bonjour*," I started tentatively.

She rose silently from her desk and, using a walker, came over to shake my hand. She wore a simple, sleeveless, white blouse under a long blazer paired with houndstooth-check cotton trousers. Her manner, like her clothes, was businesslike. Her expression was inscrutable; there was no welcome in her face or her body language. I got the impression that she didn't take me very seriously. Much later, these suspicions were confirmed. When I originally requested information about Irène, le Tarnec responded that the museum had no documentation on her. But when I read the curator's book on the de Camondo family, I found footnotes referring to letters from Irène to her children held in the museum's archives. Why had she kept them from me?

"*Bonjour. Je suis Mme Sophie le Tarnec.*"

She indicated I should sit down at a table in the middle of the room and she lowered herself into a chair kitty-corner to me. I was intimidated, not just because of her expertise. She spoke in rapid French, agreeing to a short interview before I would examine the artifacts she had pulled for me. Her voice was so soft and quavering, I had to lean in to hear every word. On the other hand, she had to do the same to understand my terrible accent. We were even.

I wished I had an interpreter. Le Tarnec either didn't speak English or chose not to do so. I had written and rehearsed all my questions in French, and I had a recorder to ensure I could replay her answers, but forming follow-up questions on the spot was almost impossible. To add to this, whatever had caused her to use a walker had played havoc with her vocal cords, and I didn't want to press her to speak more loudly or repeat things. The playback on the recorder is frequently inaudible and, while I remember the basics of what she told me, I'm not able to adequately replicate the conversation here.

I started by asking why there weren't many family photos in the house. She explained that after his son was killed, Moïse spent only about a third of his time in the house. The other two-thirds were spent travelling, buying pieces for his collection, or at the country home, Villa Béatrice, about an hour out of Paris in Aumont.[9] So my feeling that this house wasn't really a home was confirmed.

I asked about four more questions, getting succinct, unadorned, unembellished answers in response. I almost wished the curator would stand up and say, "That's all I have time for."

Through the audioguide, I had learned that Béatrice and her husband lived with Moïse after their marriage. He had divided rooms to provide an apartment for their growing family. Still I couldn't imagine trying to prevent little ones from climbing onto delicate silk-covered chairs or having to save a priceless Limoges vase as it toppled off a Louis XVI table.

"Wasn't Comte de Camondo terrified the grandchildren would break something?" I asked.

For the first time in the conversation, le Tarnec's face came alive. She explained the couple moved when the children were quite young. Then with a knowing smile, she said, *"Béatrice était très pratique,"* Her guard had dropped. She relaxed a little bit, sat back in the chair.

I hadn't intended to ask my next question, but I took advantage of le Tarnec's lowered defences. *"Pourquoi Béatrice n'a-t-elle pas échappé à Paris?"* Why hadn't she escaped? The verbal floodgates opened. I understood most of what she said as she explained that Béatrice didn't believe she was in danger. She thought only foreign-born Jews were being targeted. Le Tarnec's tone was passionate, tinged with sorrow and regret. I just shook my head.

Privilege. It lulls us into a sense of false security. And that same sort of a false sense spawned the cognitive dissonance of my post-retirement. I couldn't believe I was struggling with retirement, that I was becoming a person I didn't recognize – fearful, hesitant, filled with self-doubt. And I was ashamed at the same time. I had so much. I had no right. I could not complain. I was selfish and ungrateful.

Several moments of silence passed before the curator indicated the materials lying on the table in front of me – five photo albums starting in 1904 as well as a thick dossier containing de Camondo's will and the correspondence between Béatrice and Les Arts Decoratifs concerning the donation of her father's house and collection.

I put on cotton gloves. The smallest album was surprisingly heavy, black and leather-bound. The words "Kodak Souvenirs" were printed in gold on the front. A shadow hung over my mind as I opened the cover. I knew where this family was headed.

I'm not sure what I expected to find during this exercise. The people in the pictures weren't going to speak to me. Looking through the photos of the de Camondos was very much like going through old albums that belonged to my mother and grandmother. Pictures of people I didn't know were attached to black construction-paper pages with those funny little photo corners. Unlike our family's albums, where the glue on many of those corners had disintegrated and the pictures were sandwiched together in the centre, the de Camondo albums were pristine, perfectly archived.

I felt a little discouraged and a bit embarrassed that Mme le Tarnec's impression of me was probably accurate. I wasn't a serious scholar. I wasn't connecting in any way with the family. Until one snapshot made me gasp out loud. Le Tarnec looked up from her desk.

"*Désolé*," I said. She nodded and put her head back down. I wished I could have communicated to her what moved me. In the photo, Béatrice, around ten years old, stands beside a huge, long-haired black dog. Her gaze has the same serious contemplation Renoir captured in her mother. I went back to the beginning and looked for every snapshot that included Béatrice. She rarely smiled. Of course, I want to believe that she was affected by the divorce, or that she wasn't allowed to see her mother often enough, or that her father spent more time collecting artworks than he spent with her, but I can't convince myself. These were her father's albums and the kids look like they had a good life and a parent who wanted to capture that life. Maybe she was just a serious young girl. Bonnie always ribs me about my grade ten school picture. In it, I'm fourteen, a little bit sullen, trying to look sophisticated and world weary. It says, *If you have to take this picture, I'm going to control how the world sees me.* Was Béatrice trying to control her world?

When I finished with that album, I rested my hand on the leather cover, the cover touched by Moïse de Camondo, Nissim and Béatrice. Perhaps, when Béatrice's children were old enough, they tussled over it as they sat side-by-side on their grandfather's settee. I let the moment linger. Of the hundreds of thousands who had passed through the doors of this museum, how many had had the privilege of looking behind the display of de Camondo wealth and their tragic story to see the family's happier days frozen in time?

The remaining albums were large – about 40 x 30 cm. The first two showed Béatrice and Nissim through their teens, acting in costume dramas staged at the summer house, skating, playing tennis, golfing and riding horses together. They looked like good friends.

I had almost forgotten about Sophie le Tarnec when one of her staff asked for her assistance. I was left by myself, and it felt a little discomfiting. What if something went missing? I pushed my uneasiness aside and lifted the next album from the dwindling pile. Béatrice and Nissim were in their early twenties. I lost count of the number of photos of Béatrice on horseback. They document the many equestrian events she loved, suggesting horses were her life. I stopped at a picture of Nissim in full uniform astride a horse. He's wearing what I think of as a French Foreign Legion hat, a *kepi* with a circular flat top and a peak. He's got that confident look of young men who believe they are immortal – like the war was one great adventure. I assume his father took the picture and imagined how proud Moïse must have been. Nissim wrote regularly to his father during the war. The letters often ended with "I tenderly embrace you" before he signed them, "Nini."[10] As a parent, it's not hard to imagine Moïse's devastation on first learning that his son was missing, and then, after holding out hope, hearing he was dead.

But again, I wonder about Béatrice, the second born, the girl. How did she react to his death? Did her relationship with her father change? Although it has become kind of a joke in our family, my older brother – also the first born – held an extra special place in the family. He could do no wrong. I try to put myself in Béatrice's place. I idolized my brother, especially when I was a teenager. What does a family do after that loss?

They carry on. Beatrice's children – Moïse's grandchildren – fill the final album. Fanny and Bertrand at a beach, sitting on a donkey on the front porch of the country house, even helping to push a motorcar through town. Both children are dark haired like their mother but without her almost perpetually serious expression.

I found just one image of Béatrice's husband, a sort of dark fuzzy photo of him reading.

Only the dossier remained. As I read through the will and the information about the museum's inauguration, December 21st, 1936, I couldn't help but think it fortuitous that Moïse died at sixty-five. If he had been alive when the Nazis occupied Paris, I doubt he would have survived the war. There was no reason to save him. He collected the type of art Göring and Hitler loved; it wasn't "decadent" like the Impressionist portrait of *Little Irène* in her blue-and-white dress with a blue bow in her long, brown hair. Would his treasures have been found after the war? If so, who would have reclaimed them?

I left the archives without an escort, walking alone through the darkened museum and down the marble staircase, followed by the ghosts of the family. I wished I could leave them at the front door, but I couldn't.

Over the next few days, I tried to shake them off as I toured the Quai Branly museum, a collection of art from Africa, Asia, Oceania and the Americas, and the Rodin museum, filled with Rodin's sculptures. But the family clung to me, refusing to let go.

I realized this need to know had become something personal. Little of it could end up in a literary travel book. It had become a passion. When I started university the first time, I intended to major in history – mostly because of teachers like Mrs. Bixley. That need to understand where I am, who I am in relation to whom, and what came before me has followed me through my life.

So, the next week, at the Shoah Memorial, the de Camondos crowded into the elevator with me and pushed me through the door leading to the memorial's documentation centre.

Three other researchers were taking notes from papers spread out on the maple-coloured tables in front of them. The feeling here was so different from the BNF and not just because of the warmth of the wooden furniture and the lack of grey concrete. The silence was reverential, self-imposed. And I felt different here too. I looked at the others working on their research and felt part of them. Gone were any feelings of being an imposter. I wasn't here because of some externally imposed assignment; I was on a quest.

I knew what I was looking for – documentation about how and why Béatrice, her husband, Léon, and their children were arrested and why they weren't protected. I felt confident I would find what I was looking for, in fact looked forward to the challenge. I had made it through the most frustrating experience (getting a library card) and the most challenging situation (talking to Sophie le Tarnec).

Like Oliver Burke promised in *The Antidote*, I had embarrassed myself and I was still OK.

At the information desk, the archivist was eager to help me order the documents I had found in the memorial's online catalogue. Although she spoke perfect English, she encouraged me to use my French, and her non-threatening manner made it possible for me to do so. When I fumbled for a word, she helped me without making me feel inadequate. I filled out the required forms with her assistance and sat down to wait for the microfiched records to arrive.

I thought about Béatrice. In 1942, she renounced her Jewish faith, and like her mother, separated from her husband and was baptized Catholic. Did she become a Catholic as an insurance policy? Le Tarnec and her colleague, Nora Seni, do not think so. "*Son absence totale de clairvoyance exclut que ce fût par calcul,*" they write. (Béatrice didn't have the foresight to have calculated anything so deliberate.) They call her refusal to see the reality of the situation, "*imprudence mortelle*" (fatal carelessness).[11] What a brilliant expression. How many of us have been careless with the fates? Had too many glasses of wine before driving home, ignored the warning signs of ill health?

I thought about all those equestrian photos I had seen in the archives. Before the war, Béatrice had once hunted with Göring and, until the end of 1942, she rode every morning in the Bois de Boulogne, even took part in horse shows with German officers.[12]

Her estranged husband, Léon, could not convince her they weren't safe in occupied Paris. He moved to the unoccupied zone, where their nineteen-year-old son, Bertrand, joined him.[13] They planned to escape to Spain.

There is some debate about the date Béatrice and Fanny were arrested in Paris for not wearing their yellow stars. There is no argument about Léon and Bertrand, who were arrested in Ariège, near the Spanish border, December 12, 1942. Apparently, they were betrayed by the guide hired to lead them to Spain.[14] The whole family was interned in Drancy, the detention centre on the outskirts of Paris aptly named "the last circle before hell."[15]

Weeks later, I visited the Shoah Memorial overlooking the site of the Drancy detention centre. While I would highly recommend it, getting there required taking the métro to the suburbs and then a twenty-minute bus ride. The exhibit space is on the second floor, where I looked out onto three apartment blocks arranged in a horseshoe around a large green space. Those same apartments unfinished, without heat or running water, were used to temporarily house prisoners, mostly Jews, before deportation. A boxcar and segments of railway track remind us of the hundreds who left Drancy never to return.

I was the only one in the centre until a school class joined me. The security guard, a journalist supplementing her income who I had been chatting with for about thirty minutes, shook her head as the teachers tried to shush the students, all around fifteen years old, and the tour guide attempted to speak.

"They don't take it seriously," she said. "And they need to, or history will repeat itself." I agreed. Even as we celebrate the rights gays, lesbians and trans people have gained over forty years, we are watching many lawmakers in the USA and in countries around the world trying to claw back those rights.

∿

The archivist called me up to the counter and handed me several spools of microfiched material. The whirring of the microfiche machine broke the silence of the reading room. Countless documents slid past the screen. Within minutes, I was holding printed copies of correspondence dated from March 23 to May 15, 1943. Unlike our perfect word-processed characters, the letters on these pages wandered above and below the line. Some were almost too faint to read, as if the typewriter ribbon had been recycled one too many times. There were words I couldn't make out, and I had to remind myself these were documents written seventy years ago. It was a miracle they weren't destroyed to prevent their use in evidence.

The first letter I read requested leniency for Léon Reinach and his family. I recognized the signature, Georges Duhamel, the director of the Institute of France. Reinach's father had donated his house and contents to the Institute so it was understandable that Duhamel would write on his behalf.

The ambassador of France under the Vichy government apparently wasn't the best recipient for the request. The next letter, written to Standartenführer Helmut Knochen (the equivalent to a colonel in the Nazi secret service) includes the appeal from Duhamel, but notes that "Duhamel is known for his negative, anti-German sentiments." I reread this note several times. How often, I wondered, had French citizens turned over Jews? Then I thought about the 3,900 names on Le Mur des Justes, the wall running down the alley next to the Shoah Memorial. During the war, these people had put their lives in danger to save Jews in France. I tried to imagine myself in Paris during the occupation. Would I have been brave enough to hide Jews or help them escape? How would fear and threats have changed me? Would it have been easier to go against the Nazis as a young person? If I had been in my sixties, would I have wanted to protect my own comfort by not rocking the boat?

I turned my attention back to the letters I had printed. The next two were in German and the fuzzy, black type made them almost illegible. I opened my computer and copied the contents into Google Translate. The translation wasn't great, but I could get the sense of them.

The first summarized how Léon Reinach and his son were arrested in the unoccupied territory in Ariège, where they lived illegally. It also claims Fanny visited her father there without authorization. Reinach's behaviour in Drancy is described as "arrogant" and "brash." Deportation is recommended.[16]

The next letter, dated April 22, 1943 felt like lead in my hands: "Do not allow Léon Reinach and his family to go free and do not respond to [Duhamel's] request."[17]

I never dreamed I would physically hold a death warrant. I wanted to turn the letter over, escape from the room, lock myself in the public toilet and cry. Léon, Fanny and Bertrand were deported from

Drancy on November 20, 1943 and died that year. Béatrice survived longer because she was put in charge of the infants in Drancy, but she was deported to Auschwitz on March 7, 1944 and died January 4, 1945 – two weeks before the Russians liberated the camp.[18]

I had many more documents to order but I needed a break. I said a silent *thank you* to my mentor, Harry, who'd supported my decision to abandon my pitch and return to my original idea of a literary travel book. I had been in the documentation room for one hour, but the burden of reading the letters made me feel I had been chained to the desk for days. I wondered how my classmates managed to research difficult topics without collapsing under their weight.

I took my break in the courtyard. The warmth of the afternoon sun lifted some of the darkness from my heart. Again, I walked along the wall of names. I looked for Béatrice's mother, Irène, under Cahen d'Anvers, then Sampieri. She was not there. So many wealthy Jews escaped France. Had she done the same? And then I thought about her portrait. How had the Renoir ended up in Switzerland? The idea of repatriating stolen art had fascinated me since the discovery of 1,400 works – many believed to have been stolen from Jews – in the Munich apartment of Cornelius Gurlitt. Had the Renoir painting been part of Nazi plunder?

I took a deep breath and headed back inside. I searched the database for anything attached to the name Sampieri and almost missed the one and only document because her last name had been misspelled. On September 18, 1941, Georges Prade, a Paris city counsellor, wrote to the General Commissariat for Jewish Affairs on behalf of the Comtesse Sampierri *[sic]*. Prade requested the Comtesse's pension of 15,000 francs, which, he said, "like all Israelites, [she] has a right to." Her address was listed as 10 rue Galilée, about a kilometre from the Champs-Élysées. The letter also mentions that the Comtesse was receiving 36,000 francs per annum from her daughter, Béatrice Reinach.[19] Béatrice not only kept in touch with her mother but helped support her.

Weeks later, I reread parts of the Assouline book. My ability to read French is fairly good, but my memory is poor. I did not remember highlighting these words: during the war, "Comtesse Sampieri passed a large part of four years cloistered in an apartment on rue de La Tour."[20] Irène was in Paris for the entire war.

I thought I would follow Béatrice's story to its tragic end and, if I was lucky, learn a bit more about her mother. Now that I knew Irène had survived the occupation in Paris, I was determined to follow her story as far as I could. I was an explorer on a fascinating, albeit grim, treasure hunt.

My earlier feelings about Irène Sampieri's *chutzpah* for leaving her husband were tempered when I discovered she had stayed in Paris during the arrests and deportation of her daughter and grand-children. Did she want to help? Could she have? Maybe she tried. When I put myself in her position, I knew I'd be fighting hard to survive. She was sixty-eight at the beginning of the war, seventy-three by the time it ended. She must have been terrified. No doubt her Italian name gave her some protection from nosy neighbours because her conversion to Catholicism certainly wouldn't have guaranteed safety. Béatrice had converted, but that didn't make a difference to her.

When I first retired and started to get rejections for pitches I sent to magazines, I didn't persevere. I didn't understand that even the best writers are rejected. But they keep going. Now, I refused to let a lack of persistence or stamina stop me. I was determined to discover something about Irène's life after the war.

I asked the archivist what happened to property owned by Jews who died in the concentration camps.

"Every effort was made to find relatives," she said.

It struck me that Irène would have been Béatrice's closest family member. I knew Béatrice had inherited Villa Béatrice and her father's considerable fortune. If Irène claimed the de Camondo's summer home outside Paris, I would know she had stayed in France at least for a while after the war.

My Type A personality had its disadvantages when I was struggling with my rootlessness, but now that I was on a mission, it came in handy. If I had been in Canada, I would have known who to contact about real estate dating back to the '40s. But my lack of fluent French and my ignorance about French bureaucracy meant I was limited to using the Internet. I entered search term after search term. I'm not sure what words triggered the retrieval of a 2009 urban study of the community of Aumont-en-Halatte, the area where Villa Béatrice was located, but one part of the study highlighted famous people who had lived there. Naturally, the de Camondo family was included.[21]

Still high on the success I had had with the museum's curator, I adopted a what-the-hell attitude and emailed the communications director for the township: "When Moïse de Camondo died, his daughter Béatrice inherited the house. But when the Nazis confiscated the property, what happened to it?" I really didn't expect anything to come of it; I was writing to someone associated with a document printed five years earlier. But three days later, I received a reply from the mayor's assistant, Didier Grospiron. He attached an extract from a book called *La Longue Histoire d'Aumont-en-Halatte*, written by François Agostini, which included "The History of Villa Béatrice." He also attached a recent picture of the house. It was like winning a free ticket for the lottery – not huge, but with all sorts of potential. There was also a sense of self-satisfaction. Even though my language skills were limited, I wasn't entirely hamstrung. With a little ingenuity, I could do some butt-kicking research.

The excerpt Grospiron sent showed a generous and community-spirited Béatrice, which I welcomed after seeing the photos of an upbringing that denied her nothing in terms of material goods and opportunities. From September 1939 until May 1940, she and her husband set up a mini boarding school in the villa. Children in the region whose fathers were deployed and whose mothers had to work could stay for free. Fanny and Bertrand helped their parents with the teaching, while the house staff took care of the housekeeping and cooking duties.[22]

According to Agostini, the house was taken over by the Nazis during the war. After the war, "the mother of Mrs. Léon Reinach sold Villa Béatrice." Irène Sampieri, having survived the war, became the sole heir to her daughter Béatrice's fortune and sold the property in 1948 to the SNCF, the national rail service.[23]

I'd like to think Béatrice would have been happy with that; after all, she had been giving her mother an allowance, maybe in secret so her father wouldn't know. I was delighted that the property and money didn't automatically revert to the state, especially since I feel the Vichy government had to take some responsibility for the treatment of France's Jewish population. But I imagine Moïse de Camondo would have been outraged. Irène had run off with another man and shamed the family name with her divorce and her conversion to Catholicism.

There was just one piece left to Irène's story. How did the Renoir portrait of her as a child end up in Switzerland? At some point – none of the biographers seems to know exactly when – Béatrice was given the portrait of her mother. Maybe it was a housewarming gift when she and Léon moved into their first apartment, or maybe it was bequeathed to her when her grandmother died.

However she got it, I found a reference to it in my search through the Shoah Memorial's database in a letter dated 1941. At the beginning of the war, many private Jewish art collectors entrusted their treasures to Jacques Jaujard, the director of national museums. He was the person responsible for hiding the treasures of the Louvre so Hitler couldn't steal them. He distributed the works from the Louvre and from private collections to various *châteaux* around the countryside. In the letter, Béatrice's husband asks that same Jaujard to help him get back "specifically the Renoir portrait of the mother of my wife, née Béatrice de Camondo." Of course, he was referring to *Mademoiselle Irène Cahen d'Anvers (Little Irène)*. [24]

This really was a treasure hunt, and I was loving the challenge of following a trail of half-eaten breadcrumbs. I searched online records of Nazi plunder compiled by historian Patricia Kennedy Grimsted. They show seizures from the Château de Chambord on July 7, 1940. Léon Reinach's name appears on that list. The contents are not itemized, but *Little Irène* was likely in one of the two cases taken.[25] I was so mesmerized by this story, I actually bought Nancy Yeide's *Beyond the Dreams of Avarice*, a huge 2.6 kg volume (I weighed it) that lists the artworks stolen by those working for the Nazis. According to her research, the Renoir painting was confiscated from Béatrice and

Léon. Then, in 1942, it was given to Gustav Rochlitz, a German art dealer living in Paris, in exchange for a Florentine *tondo* (a traditional Italian circular painting).[26] *Little Irène* was recovered in 1945 by the Monuments, Fine Arts, and Archives Program (MFAAP, on which the 2014 film, The Monuments Men, was loosely based). In 1946, it was part of a Paris exhibition of artworks recovered from Germany.

On my final visit to the Shoah Memorial, I ordered only one document, the catalogue for that 1946 exhibition: *Les Chefs-d'Œuvre des collections privées françaises retrouvées en Allemagne.* There was no whirring microfiche machine, no clunking printer. I held the original. My hands shook. The cover was dog-eared, the spine torn. The plain white paper had yellowed with age. As I opened the small booklet to page seventeen, I imagined a visitor holding this catalogue in her hands, first reading the description, then looking up at painting number 41 RENOIR – *Mlle Irène Cahen d'Anvers.*

The final page of the catalogue makes this disclaimer: "Because of the exceptional circumstances under which this exhibition was organized, it isn't possible to indicate the owners of these masterpieces." It didn't take long before at least one owner stepped forward to reclaim a painting. Did Irène Sampieri see the portrait by accident, or did someone tell her it was there? The restitution took two years and, in 1949, having squandered much of the de Camondo fortune (apparently on gambling) Irène sold her portrait for 240,000 Swiss francs, (about $55,000 US). The buyer was Emil Bührle, a Swiss industrialist who bought artworks stolen from Jews and sold arms to the Nazis.[27]

When I turned my back on the Shoah Memorial, I left the de Camondos to rest in peace. I had walked beside them for part of their journey, but now it was time to return to the present.

I held on to this story, a compelling chapter in Paris's past, which helped me step up and take control in a task I believed was beyond me. As I walked out into the cool autumn air I was overcome by a sense of satisfaction and a resolve and confidence I had not known in a long time.

CHAPTER 9

FROM WINTER TO SPRING: THE SEARCH FOR SELF CONTINUES

Graduation drew us together in Halifax like iron filings around the magnetic north. First Suzanne, who was showing her parents and brothers the King's library. Then Jeff, sporting a full head of hair and a hipster beard. Andrew was alone. He and his wife had recently had a baby, and she was back in Toronto. Even Harry came up from his home in Amherst to be with us.

As we waited for the official photo, I took on the job of pinning hoods to gowns, dresses and shirts. Designed to sit underneath a tie, the band on the front of the hood comes with a loop that hooks over a shirt button (obviously with males in mind). These days men don't often wear ties – thus the need for safety pins. The excitement amongst the grads was tangible, but I had mixed emotions about bringing this part of my reinvention full circle.

∼

Back in 1976 when my first teaching job included a full slate of English classes, I knew I needed some actual qualifications. I had squeaked out a B minus on the single English course listed on my science degree transcript. So, when I graduated with an MA in

English language and literature almost ten years into my career it was a very big deal.

But here's the sad reality. It didn't make me a better teacher, except maybe for the top senior students who were planning to study literature in university. I thought I'd be better. I knew more about Milton. I had written publishable scholarly papers. This is how much my head was stuck in the university world. I actually photocopied the First Folio edition of *The Tempest* to use in my Shakespeare class. I was eager for my students to know the impact typesetters in the 1600s had on what we read in our modern texts. After all, I reasoned in the glow of my shiny new English MA, who wouldn't be absolutely fascinated by kerning, bad quartos and plagiarism?

That MA didn't make me better. Would this MFA in Creative Non-fiction change anything?

~

The official photographer gathered us onto the steps outside the library. Black gowns fluttered like crows' wings as graduates passed purses and bouquets of flowers to parents, friends partners and rushed to join their classmates. Our class almost missed the group shot while we waited for latecomers.

We were only ten of eighteen graduates from the program. Some couldn't justify the cost of the flight for a dinner and a three-hour ceremony. Others were dealing with family or work issues. One was on holiday overseas.

At the graduation dinner the previous evening, speakers praised the parents for their roles in their sons' and daughters' successes. They applauded King's for preparing their students to stride confidently into their futures, for producing full-feathered fledglings capable of facing the challenges of precipitous heights and buffeting winds that would surely meet us as we left the nest.

The longer they spoke, the older and more disenfranchised I felt. I should have been paying more attention. I imagined when graduation was over, I would arrive – somewhere – not be getting started, not be worrying about how strong my wings were.

I hadn't looked past putting on the gown and hood. I *was* a fledgling and no doubt would suffer some cuts and bruises as I fell out of the nest. Even though I had learned an amazing amount about the publishing industry and about writing, the reality was I didn't even have a finished manuscript. It would take two years post-graduation to be able to put into perspective the idea that getting my degree was only a bus stop along my life-ride.

The ceremony was filled with pomp and circumstance. We paraded down University Avenue – an ostentation of peacocks with our brightly coloured hoods flowing behind us. People stopped on the street to watch us pass.

I knew Bonnie had arrived two hours early at the Cathedral Church of All Saints, and I imagined her in the front row, camera poised. Inside the church hall, we were marshalled into our graduating classes in alphabetical order to guarantee we received the correct diploma. Our group was last. We processed through the front doors of the church and under the soaring wooden gothic arches toward our seats set up in the arms of the transept. Cameras clicked on all sides. Bonnie stood in the third row on the aisle. She pointed the camera, shot, then waved and blew me a kiss. There was such pride in her face.

My throat constricted.

In the '80s, Bonnie and I went to see two of our favourite lesbian singers at Carnegie Hall. In her introduction to one of her songs, Meg Christian said, "I have spent an incredible amount of energy waiting for X to happen. When this thing happens, everything is going to be OK." When I finished my degree, I assumed my retirement reinvention would be "complete," that the accomplishment would somehow transform me. It was the "X" I had been waiting for.

In *The Subtle Art of Not Giving a F*ck*, a book I reread often, author Mark Manson observes, "Happiness is not a solvable equation."[1]

My throat constriction as I looked at Bonnie, so lovingly, proudly taking my photo, was probably a reaction to the subtly creeping notion that reinvention doesn't have an end point. It happens constantly. I wasn't "done." I realized I had measured my success in terms of completing a manuscript and getting that degree – that external recognition. Standing under those gothic arches in the church, surrounded by proud parents and proud graduates, I had one of those ah-ha moments. When someone handed me my large navy blue folder with that precious piece of parchment in it, all those things I learned in the streets, graveyards and galleries in Paris would become even more important. Those lessons, along with many more I was sure I would learn, were going to support me through the next twenty years, help me to make the most of what was left of my life.

And a piece of parchment wasn't going to make problems go away. Everyone has problems. "Problems add a sense of meaning and importance to our life," Manson says. "To duck our problems is to lead a meaningless (even if supposedly pleasant) existence."[2]

My whole retirement reinvention was triggered by my sense of failure. I measured my retirement in terms of some external definition of success. I failed at things I wanted to be good at, and I certainly was not as successful at reaching my initial goals as Bonnie seemed to be. Instead of confronting these problems, it was less challenging to avoid, to hide in the security of daily, obsessive, repetitive and distracting activities, appearing to be busy and content.

It's much easier now, with over two years' perspective, to understand Meg Christian's song which says that whatever makes us happy comes from within. Waiting for something outside myself was not going to do it.

I've recently started volunteering with a literacy organization, not because the gurus say it's something we should do in retirement to make us feel useful to the next generation, but because it makes me feel good.

Do we retirees sometimes set ourselves up for failure? I believe so. In North America we are rewarded for a strong work ethic, being industrious and productive in our jobs. In 1986, sociologist David Ekerdt coined the phrase "busy ethic," an extension of the work ethic that follows us into retirement.[3]

I've said it before, but the worst question asked of retirees is "What are you going to do?" The underlying message is that success in retirement is measured by "doing." Those who fall into the "busy ethic" trap feel they have to be "doing things" in retirement or, if still working, be planning to "do things." Ekerdt says, "Exactly what one does to keep busy is secondary to the fact that one purportedly is busy."[4] If we're not doing something, we think we've failed. But doing things for no other reason than to be busy is avoiding confronting who we are and what we want in our retirement. I could have been the "busy ethic" poster woman.

The quest for reinvention has made me understand I shouldn't find things to do just to avoid feeling lost or down. It's OK to have bad days, even bad weeks, as long as I can figure out what is causing my anxieties, my fears – to be brave enough to stay in the moment, look deeply into my emotions and not skim over them. It's not unlike Sister Wendy teaching me to spend time with a painting, to walk away but then to come back. Or the Buddhist monk who advocates experiencing life as it happens by focusing on exactly what is going on in that moment.

With age and maturity comes an understanding of who we are. Few of us would like to go back to our teens and twenties when we were still searching for our identities. But what retirement can do is unsettle us – throw us back to the way we felt when we were young. Manson writes, "Anything that shakes up [our] comfort – even if it could potentially make [our lives] better – is inherently scary."[5]

Security. After thirty-one years in education, I knew who I was. I was a wife, a mom and a grandmother. I was a teacher, writer, singer, skier, traveller. I have been many things in my life, including a motorcycle instructor. But retirement still set me back. Like my skin, which sags with age, I lost the life flexibility I had when I was younger.

Looking back, it was far more than losing the identity I had. I think the biggest mistake I made was imagining a new and specific identity for myself in retirement. I was going to be A WRITER. When I talked about Paris, I said I was going to be like Hemingway and become a *flâneuse*. What a way to set myself up for failure. In my mind, writers were a small group of people breathing rarefied air, the Margaret Atwoods and Alice Munros of the world.

Manson suggests, "The narrower and rarer the identity you choose for yourself the more everything will seem to threaten you."[6] With my lofty goal, putting myself in a box called "writer," came an entire set of criteria for success. "How many articles have you published? What publications have accepted your work?" And after the MFA, it was almost worse. "Who have you submitted your manuscript to? Have you got an agent? What's your next book?"

Yikes.

Very early in this process, I read *Happy Retirement: The Psychology of Reinvention*. Kenneth Schultz, one of four contributors, was the one who suggested taking up one of the arts, but only for the intrinsic rewards it brought. Bonnie always said she wanted to see how far she could push herself with her art, find out how good she could be. But she never measured herself against others, only against herself. That's not to say she doesn't look at a Bouguereau with admiration and probably a bit of envy. And she is always blown away by the fine quality of the artists in the courses she takes, both the instructors and students. But instead of thinking, "I'll never be as good as they are," she asks, "What can I learn from them?" And then she gets out her pencils or paints and tries to figure out what she needs to do to continue improving.

Two years after graduating, I've put these past five years of trying to reinvent myself into perspective. I'm not what I do. I'm still practicing yoga and walking – though not so obsessively. I watch television that inspires me, makes me laugh or leaves me on the edge of my seat. I read – a lot.

And as for writing, I haven't stopped; in fact, I've got some fun projects on the go. But I'm trying to emulate Héloïse, altering the way I see that part of my life. I've stopped putting so much emphasis on the goal of publishing, instead focusing on my love of finding unusual stories. Some of them might be worthy of a pitch; others will just be good fodder for chatting with friends in the coffee shop or over dinner.

I may not write formally for the rest of my life, but I'll collect experiences, see stories everywhere I go, and I'm never going to give up looking for a good yarn.

I am not at the end of my search for self. I am not a finished piece of work. In retirement, I am still "becoming."

END NOTES

CHAPTER 1 NOTES

1. Ernie J. Zelinski, *How to Retire Happy, Wild, and Free: Retirement Wisdom That You Won't Get From Your Financial Advisor* (Edmonton: Visions International Publishing, 2016).
2. Nancy K. Schlossberg, *Revitalizing Retirement: Reshaping your Identity, Relationships, and Purpose* (Washington: American Psychological Association, 2009; Kindle Edition, Location 303).
3. Jamie Chamberlin, "Retiring Minds Want to Know," *Monitor* 45, no. 1 (January 2014): http://www.apa.org/monitor/2014/01/retiring-minds.aspx.

CHAPTER 2 NOTES

1. Bernard Pascuito (with Stéphanie Lohr), *Dalida, une vie brûlée* (Paris: Archipoche, 2007; Kindle Edition, Location 89). Note: Author's translations.
2. Paul Kennedy, "You Are Here," *Ideas* 1.2967484 (CBC Radio: February 23, 2015; Location 7:26).
3. Alex Hutchinson, "Global Impositioning Systems: Is GPS Technology Actually Harming Our Sense of Direction?" *The Walrus* (November 12, 2009, updated August 4, 2016): https://thewalrus.ca/global-impositioning-systems/.
4. Lin Edwards, "Study Suggests Reliance on GPS May Reduce Hippocampus Function as We Age," *Medical Xpress* (November 18, 2010): http://phys.org/news/2010-11-reliance-gps-hippocampus-function-age.html.
5. "Cimetière-de-Montmartre," Paris: Official Website of the Convention and Visitors Bureau: https://en.parisinfo.com/paris-museum-monument/71184/Cimetiere-de-Montmartre.

6. Oliver Burkeman, *The Antidote: Happiness for People Who Can't Stand Positive Thinking* (Toronto: Penguin Canada, 2012; Kindle Edition, Location 389).
7. Burkeman, Location 536.
8. Pascuito, *Dalida,* Location 993.
9. Catherine Rihoit (with Orlando), *Dalida* (Paris: Plon, 1995), 40. Note: Author's translations.
10. Michael Rossato Bennett, *Alive Inside: A Story of Music and Memory* (documentary film), (Pottsdown, PN: MVD Entertainment Group, 2014): https://www.aliveinside.org/film.
11. Lisa J. Lehmberg and C. Victor Fung, "Benefits of Music Participation for Senior Citizens: A Review of the Literature," *Music Education Research International* 4 (2010), 21: http://cmer.arts.usf.edu/content/articlefiles/3122-MERI04pp.19-30.pdf p. 21.
12. Rihoit, *Dalida,* 406.
13. Megan Kaye, Kenneth S. Schultz, and Mike Annesley, *Happy Retirement:The Psychology of Reinvention* (New York: Penguin Random House, 2016; Kindle Edition, Location 593).

CHAPTER 3 NOTES

1. Philippe Mellot, *La Vie Secrète de Montmartre* (Paris: Presses de la Cité, Omnibus Edition, 2008). Note: Author's translations.
2. Sue Roe, *The Private Lives of the Impressionists* (New York: Harper Collins, 2006; Kindle Edition) 164–65.
3. Biography.com Editors, "Henri de Toulouse-Lautrec Biography," (A&E Television Networks, April 2, 2014, updated April 12, 2019): https://www.biography.com/artist/henri-de-toulouse-lautrec.
4. www.Paris.fr, "L'Inspection générale des carrières : Un peu d'histoire" (article), "Tout savoir sur les sous sols" (webpage): https://www.paris.fr/services-et-infos-pratiques/urbanisme-et-architecture/sous-sol/tout-savoir-sur-les-sous-sols-2317#l-inspection-generale-des-carrieres_4. This page gives information about the geology of Montmartre.
5. Dupuy Georges, "Paris croule-t-il?" Lexpress.fr, June 17, 1999: https://www.lexpress.fr/informations/paris-croule-t-il_634113.html. This article tells of various places (houses and roads) around the city that have collapsed, as a result of the mines below them.
6. Elizabeth Winter, "Cotton Club of Harlem (1923–)," BlackPast.org: http://www.blackpast.org/aah/cotton-club-harlem-1923.
7. William A. Shack, *Harlem in Montmartre: A Paris Jazz Story between the Great Wars* (Berkeley: University of California Press, 2001; Kindle Edition, Location 488).

8. Shack, *Harlem in Montmartre,* Location 504.
9. Barbara Strauch, *The Secret Life of the Grown-up Brain: The Surprising Talents of the Middle-Aged Mind* (New York: Viking, 2010) 31.
10. Strauch, *Grown-up Brain*, 34.
11. Strauch, *Grown-up Brain*, 36.
12. Ibid.
13. Strauch, *Grown-up Brain*, 37.
14. Ibid.
15. Colin G. DeYoung, Jacob B. Hirsh, Matthew S. Shane, Xenophon Papademetris, Nallakkandi Rajeevan and Jeremy R. Gray, "Testing Predictions From Personality Neuroscience: Brain Structure and the Big Five," *Psychological Science* 21, no. 6 (2010): 820–28.
16. Eleonora Guglielman, "The Ageing Brain: Neuroplasticity and Lifelong Learning," eLearning Papers, no. 29 (June 2012): https://ec.europa.eu/eip/ageing/library/ageing-brain-neuroplasticity-and-lifelong-learning_en.
17. Église Saint-Jean-de-Montmartre: http://lartnouveau.com/artistes/bigot/19_rue_des_abbesses.htm.

CHAPTER 4 NOTES

1. Amanda Enayati, "The Aging Brain: Why Getting Older Just Might Be Awesome," Edition.cnn.com, June 19, 2012: http://edition.cnn.com/2012/06/19/health/enayati-aging-brain-innovation/.
2. "Bill Moyers in Conversation with Sister Wendy," YouTube.ca, June 12, 2011: https://www.youtube.com/playlist?list=PL8A29239DB60A5C59.
3. Ibid.
4. Paul Mitchell, "Pushor Mitchell Okanagan Symposium on Brain Health on May 12, 2016," Pushor Mitchell LLP: https://www.pushormitchell.com/2016/03/pushor-mitchell-presents-the-okanagan-symposium-on-brain-health-may-12-2016/.
5. Barbara Strauch "How to Train the Aging Brain" *New York Times* Dec. 29, 2009 http://www.nytimes.com/2010/01/03/education/edlife/03adult-t.html?_r=0.
6. Kaye, Schultz, and Annesley, *Happy Retirement*, Location 3079.

CHAPTER 5 NOTES

1. Lauren A. Leotti, Sheena S. Iyengar, and Kevin N. Ochsner, "Born to Choose: The Origins and Value of the Need for Control," *Trends in Cognitive Science* 14, no. 10 (October 2010): https://www.ncbi.nlm.nih.gov/pmc/articles/PMC2944661/.

2. Thomas Crook, "This Is How Your Brain Reacts To Losing A Loved One," Prevention.com, November 3, 2011: https://www.prevention.com/health/memory/a20441690/how-your-brain-reacts-to-grief/.

3. "Fans mark Jim Morrison's death," http://www.cnn.com/2001/SHOWBIZ/Music/07/10/morrison.anniversary/.

4. Catherine Hartley and Elizabeth Phelps, "Changing Fear: The Neurocircuitry of Emotion Regulation," *Neuropsychopharmacology* 35, no. 1 (2010): http://www.ncbi.nlm.nih.gov/pubmed/19710632.

5. Durant Imboden, "Père Lachaise Cemetery," Paris for Visitors: http://europeforvisitors.com/paris/articles/pere-lachaise-cemetery.htm.

6. Douglas Keister, *Stories in Stone: A Field Guide to Paris Cemeteries and Their Residents* (Utah: Gibbs Smith, 2013; Kindle Edition, Location 173).

7. Keister, *Stories in Stone*, Location 170–77.

8. Constant J. Mews, *The Lost Love Letters of Héloïse and Abelard* (New York: St. Martin's Press, 1999) 207.

9. Mews, Lost Love Letters, 209.

10. Pierre Bayle, "Letter I. Abelard to Philintus," *Project Gutenberg's Letters of Abelard and Héloïse*, trans. by John Hughes (Gutenberg Online Edition, EBook #35977, released April 27, 2011): http://www.gutenberg.org/files/35977/35977-h/35977-h.htm#a_CHI.

11. Pierre Abelard and Héloïse, *The Love Letters of Abelard and Héloïse*, ed. by Israel Gollancz and Honor Morten, trans. by Betty Radice (Santa Cruz, CA: Evinity Publishing Inc, 2009; Kindle Edition, Location 162).

12. Bayle, "Letter II. Héloïse to Abelard," *Letters of Abelard and Héloïse*.

13. Abelard and Héloïse, *Love Letters*, Location 194.

14. Abelard and Héloïse, *Love Letters*, Location 757.

15. Bayle, "Letter V. Héloïse to Abelard," *Letters of Abelard and Héloïse*.

16. Bayle, "Letter II. Héloïse to Abelard," *Letters of Abelard and Héloïse*.

17. Alistair Horne, *Seven Ages of Paris* (New York: Vintage Books, 2004) 250.

18. Horne, C266.

19. Christina Gridley and Carolyn Kemp, "Women in the Paris Commune," *In Defense of Marxism* (March 8, 2012): https://www.marxist.com/women-in-the-paris-commune.htm.

20. John Merriman, *Massacre: The Life and Death of the Paris Commune* (New York: Basic Books, 2014) 66.

21. Horne, Seven Ages of Paris, 274.
22. Adam Gopnik, "The Fires of Paris: Why Do People Still Fight About the Paris Commune?" newyorker.com, December 15, 2014: https://www.newyorker.com/magazine/2014/12/22/fires-paris.
23. L'Office Universitaire de Recherche Socialiste, "Suzanne Buisson (1883–1944)," http://www.lours.org/archives/default34f6.html?pid=904.

CHAPTER 6 NOTES

1. Pauline Rose Clance and Suzanne Imes, "The Imposter Phenomenon in High Achieving Women: Dynamics and Therapeutic Intervention," Psychotherapy: Theory, Research & Practice 15, no. 3 (Fall 1978) 6: http://www.paulineroseclance.com/pdf/ip_high_achieving_women.pdf.
2. Evelyn Kalinosky, "Feeling Like A Fraud: Living With Impostor Syndrome," forbes.com (February 22, 2010): http://www.forbes.com/2010/02/22/imposter-syndrome-professional-fraud-forbeswoman-leadership-psychology.html.
3. Kirsten Weir, "Feel Like a Fraud?" gradPSYCH 11, no. 4 (November 2013): http://www.apa.org/gradpsych/2013/11/fraud.aspx.
4. Strauch, Grown-up Brain, 72.
5. James Z. Chadick, Theodore P. Zanto and Adam Gazzaley, "Structural and Functional Differences in Medial Prefrontal Cortex Underlie Distractibility and Suppression Deficits in Ageing," Nature Communications (June 30, 2014): https://www.nature.com/articles/ncomms5223.
6. Kaye, Schultz, and Annesley, Happy Retirement, Location 420.
7. Joseph Burgo, "The Narcissistic Injury of Middle Age," theatlantic.com (February 12, 2014): http://www.theatlantic.com/health/archive/2014/02/the-narcissistic-injury-of-middle-age/283602/.

CHAPTER 7 NOTES

1. "Samuel Beckett Biography (1906–1989)," biography.com: http://www.biography.com/people/samuel-beckett-9204239#synopsis.
2. Pierre Assouline, Le Dernier des Camondo (Paris: Gallimard, 1999) 294.

CHAPTER 8 NOTES

1. Adam Gopnik, *Paris to the Moon* (New York: Random House, 2000; Kindle Edition) 185.
2. Gopnik, *Paris to the Moon*, 186.
3. Ibid.
4. Mo Costandi, "Am I Too Old to Learn a New Language?" guardian.com (September 13, 2014): http://www. theguardian.com/education/2014/sep/13/am-i-too-old-to-learn-a-language.
5. Gopnik, *Paris to the Moon*, 186.
6. Assouline, *Le Dernier des Camondo*, 234.
7. Nora Seni and Sophie le Tarnec, *Les Camondo ou l'éclipse d'une fortune* (Arles: Hébraïca, 1997) 206.
8. Assouline, *Le Dernier des Camondo*, 235.
9. Seni and le Tarnec, *Les Camondo*, 212.
10. Ibid., 238.
11. Ibid., 267.
12. Ibid.
13. Ibid., and XLVI-484/490 "Ensemble de 7 documents, datés du 24 mars 1943 au 15/05/1943, concernant Léon Reinach." Archives, Document administratif, Correspondance officielle.
14. Assouline, *Le Dernier des Camondo*, 315.
15. Seni and le Tarnec, *Les Camondo*, 267.
16. XLVI-484/490 "Ensemble de 7 documents, datés du 24 mars 1943 au 15/05/1943, concernant Léon Reinach." Archives, Document administratif, Correspondance officielle.
17. Ibid.
18. Assouline, *Le Dernier des Camondo*, 316–17.
19. #CXVI-113 "Lettre du 18/09/1941 du service de Georges Prade, conseiller municipal à Paris, adressée à Xavier Vallat, commissaire général aux questions juives, lui demandant l'autorisation pour la Comtesse de Sampierri, qui est juive, de recevoir la pension qui lui est faite en plus de la mensualité fixée par les règlements," Correspondance officielle.
20. Assouline, Le Dernier des Camondo, 318.
21. http://www.parc-oise-paysdefrance.fr/files/pnr_oise/etudes%20 urbaines/eu%20aumont.pdf p.85
22. François Agostini, *La Longue Histoire d'Aumont-En-Halatte* (Le Verguier, France: L'Association les Amis d'Aumont, 1978) 111–12.
23. Email from Didier Grospiron, adjoint au Maire d'Aumont-en-Halatte October 2, 2014; and Agostini, *La Longue Histoire*, 112–13.

24. #CCXI-39 _ 002 "Lettre du 10/08/1941 de Léon Reinach, héritier des Camondo, au directeur des musées nationaux.

25. Patricia Kennedy Grimsted, *Reconstructing the Record of Nazi Cultural Plunder: A Survey of the Dispersed Archives of the Einsatzstab Reichsleiter Rosenberg (ERR)* (Amsterdam: IISH Research Papers, 2011) Paper 47, A1–36: http://www.iisg.nl/publications/errsurvey/errsurvey_france-111019.pdf.

26. Nancy H. Yeide, *Beyond the Dreams of Avarice: The Hermann Goering Collection* (Dallas: Laurel Publishing, 2009) 466.

27. Lukas Gloor, "The Emil Bührle Collection: Works of International Artists – The Complete List," (Provenance of Auguste Renoir's Portrait de Mademoiselle Irène Cahen d'Anvers, 1880 [La petite Irène]): https://www.buehrle.ch/fileadmin/user_upload/bilder/stiftung/bestandliste/BestandEGBengl.pdf.

CHAPTER 9 NOTES

1. Mark Manson, *The Subtle Art of Not Giving a F*ck: A Counterintuitive Approach to Living a Good Life* (San Francisco: Harper One [ebook] 2016) 26.

2. Manson, *The Subtle Art of Not Giving a F*ck*, 84.

3. Harry R. Moody, *Aging: Concepts And Controversies*, 5th Ed. (Thousand Oaks, CA: Pine Forge Press, 2006) 256.

4. Ibid.

5. Manson, *The Subtle Art of Not Giving a F*ck*, 136.

6. Manson, *The Subtle Art of Not Giving a F*ck*, 140.

ACKNOWLEDGEMENTS

I would not have started on this writing journey without attending the MFA in Creative Non-fiction at the University of Kings College. Special thanks to my mentors **Harry Thurston** and **Tim Falconer** and to **Stephen Kimber** who mentored us in many informal ways and who keeps us up to date with all the news.

Two special women played a major role in this adventure. **Jane Silcott** mentor, editor and friend, your feedback, professionalism, encouragement and support went above and beyond. You believed in me when I didn't. Thank you. **Lesley Buxton,** our weekly meetings keep me sane. You are an inspiring writing buddy. Your invaluable input made me a better writer.

Mark Taylor, you are a creative giant. You are skilled, perceptive and generous. Your design has made this book a beautiful thing.

My readers – **Lore Burns, Jan Johnson, Cathryn Wellner** and **Carl Hanson** – spent hours reading, meeting and giving me feedback. Thank you for taking the time to think and respond in such a thoughtful and caring manner. Your input was honest and appreciated. Carl, thank you for rereading the book so many times and completing the initial proofreading. And Cathryn, an additional thanks for taking me through the self-publishing maze and for your constantly positive outlook.

To fellow students **Suzanne Stewart, Jeff Elliot** and **Lauren McKeon,** your help and encouragement were invaluable.

Lynne Melcombe, fellow MFA grad and proofreader extraordinaire, thank you.

Bonnie Sheppard, you are the love of my life. You inspire me every day. You took me to Paris and look what happened. Thank you for sticking with me through this process. Your cover art expresses the love we both have for Paris in winter.

CPSIA information can be obtained
at www.ICGtesting.com
Printed in the USA
BVHW030915020619
549386BV00008B/3/P